The Heart of Relationship

Five Ultimate Truths
For Understanding the Couple Relationship

Twenty-Five Suggestions
For Making Your Relationship Work

The Heart of Relationship

Five Ultimate Truths
For Understanding the Couple Relationship

Twenty-Five Suggestions
For Making Your Relationship Work

By

Jonathan Goodman-Herrick LCSW

Forward by Jan Chozen Bays, M.D.

ISBN NUMBER: 1-58500-983-0

This book is printed on acid free paper

1st Books-rev. 09/25/02

"A delightful, profoundly sage, practical book that will help any couple find their way." Hal Stone, Ph.D. and Sidra Stone, Ph.D., authors of Embracing Your Selves.

About the Book

The Heart of Relationship delineates five essential truths that underlie all couplehood: the inescapable fact of struggling and suffering, the fundamental cause of struggle and suffering, and the three evolutionary steps out of struggle and suffering. These three steps are awareness, self-care, and the twin capacity for personal power and selflessness.

Straight-forward, elegant, and entertaining, *The Heart of Relationship* is based on almost twenty years of the author's work with couples and thirty years of his own marriage.

Dedication

For Pearlyn, my wife, my life's partner, and my great joy.

Acknowledgments

It is a pleasure to acknowledge my parents, Bill and Jeannette, whose fifty-year marriage has been a wonderful role-model and inspiration; Hal and Sidra Stone, my mentors, therapists, and friends, whose work has greatly enhanced my understanding of primary relationship; and Bonnie Summers, whose over-all support helped in the writing of this book.

Table of Contents

Table of Contents

Table of Contents

PERSONAL POWER & SELFLESSNESS IN
RELATIONSHIP

CONCLUSION

Forward

Attention gives life to anything it is turned upon. Complete attention allows us to probe into the mysteries of life. In *The Heart of Relationship* Jonathan Goodman-Herrick has turned the searchlight of attention on the rich tapestry of relationship. With its five essential truths that underlie all relationship, the work is a form of meditation on couples. At the same time, it offers twenty-five wonderfully practical suggestions couples can rely on to guide them on their journey.

Both dynamic and eminently pragmatic, the wisdom distilled here emerges out of Jonathan's wide clinical experience and deep personal reflection. Using clear, compelling examples from his clinical work as well as a wealth of personal experience, he depicts relationship as a many-faceted diamond. In progressive steps, and with the support of simple exercises, *The Heart of Relationship* provides a clear, incisive overview of most key subjects couples deal with and delivers a broad view of the inner workings of marriage.

In a world over-filled with information this book is perfect. It is compact, with each page packed with valuable material. Couples will find it easy to read and readily adaptable to their unique situation. It also makes an excellent workbook for therapists to follow with clients. Flexibly organized, the book allows a therapist to direct a couple to the section most appropriate to their particular concerns. As important, the text is succinct enough that the couple might even read it! (Something I find that many couples will not do with more complex homework assignments.) Reading this book can help alter the direction a relationship will take. It also makes the whole journey far more enriching.

Jan Chozen Bays, M.D., FAAP, Zen teacher and Abbot of Larch Mountain Zen Center, author of *To Heal the Human World.*

Preface

> *For one human being to love another: that is perhaps the most difficult of all our tasks, the ultimate, the last test and proof, the work for which all other work is but preparation.*
> Rainer Maria Rilke, *Letters to a Young Poet.*

From the beginning of love, through the passing of the years, five truths describe and explain the world of committed, intimate relationship. When everything else is stripped away from the confusion and stories surrounding the life of a couple, five truths remain.

These principles lead developmentally from one to the next.

The first truth is that relationship, by its very nature, consists of struggle and suffering.

The second truth is that our fundamental fear and need are the cause of struggle and suffering in relationship. On the psychological or human level these underlie everything else: fear and need drive us; and fear and need drive relationship.

The third truth is that all efforts to resolve struggle and suffering begin with awareness: awareness of our needs and fears and of how we interact in relationship. A key element of awareness is the development of emotional literacy: learning how to read our own feelings and mental processes.

The fourth truth is that self-care, the compassionate tending of our own neediness and fearfulness, of our over-all vulnerability, is essential to genuine, healthy interaction.

The final truth is that the ultimate capacity for deeply satisfying relationship is a seeming paradox: it is the capacity to manifest personal power in combination with genuine selflessness.

The third, fourth and fifth principles of love all point to the way out of struggle and suffering.

Through greater awareness, self-care, and ultimately dynamic personal power and selflessness, we slowly move out of struggle and suffering into an unsurpasasable fulfillment and joy.

Although it sometimes seems that we are making absolutely no headway in our couple relationship, the very commitment to successful relationship leads us, inch by inch, away from struggle towards personal power and selflessness. This is because no matter what other, more comfortable strategies we try, nothing else works. As a couple we are two creatures in a cosmic maze: we keep running down different pathways, such as the anger pathway, the blame pathway, the pathway of force, the avoidance pathway, the emotional bribery pathway, the shutting down pathway, the running away pathway, and the pathway of fantasizing another partner. But the only passageways that lead out of relationship suffering and struggle are the passageways of awareness, of self-care, and of personal power and selflessness.

****

The modern view of couples, derived in part from understanding computers, is that couples are a system or loop, where one partner's condition directly affects the other's: if one partner is depressed or having an affair it is not an isolated incident but relates to the other's behavior or emotional configuration. Partners are not two islands but two points on a single circuit. One practical application is that a couple therapist can intervene with either partner to affect the couple as a whole, or intervene with the couple as a whole to heal one partner. However when couples attempt to *fix* themselves, each half generally tries to get the other to change, which only produces resistance. The reader is encouraged to see relationship as a single loop – but a loop where the most effective point of entry for change is yourself. Change yourself and you change your partner. This book helps understand how to do that.

****

The Heart of Relationship is divided into two parts. The first section, *Five Ultimate Truths,* explores the truths mentioned above; it includes anecdotes from my work with clients and some from my own marriage. The second section, *Twenty-five Suggestions,* is a series of very specific recommendations that take these truths into account. These suggestions incorporate every emotional tool I have ever found useful in clearing my own way and in guiding others to clear their way through the vines and thickets of intimate partnership. Each suggestion concludes with an exercise or series of questions to consider.

My hope is that this work illuminates the very difficult, very wonderful journey of loving partnership wherever, along the way, the reader may be.

Introduction: Innocent Tourists

> The greatest danger, that of losing one's own self may pass off quietly as if it were nothing; every other loss, that of an arm, a leg, five dollars, is sure to be noticed.Soren Kierkegaard, *Either/Or.*

Many of us assume, with disastrous consequences, that the great wilderness of relationship is merely a Disney creation. Innocent tourists, we think that once we buy our ticket, in most case's the wedding ceremony, the ride will take care of itself. We assume it is going to be a safe, pleasant, basically care-free, straight-forward passage, a trip we can just sit-back-and-enjoy. We forget that true adventure and safety are mutually exclusive.

It reminds me of a trip my family and I took to Costa Rica a few years ago.

This tropical land is an especially lovely, politically civilized country which, I think, contributed to our making plans as if we were visiting a US resort. Soon after leaving the modern, international airport in San Jose, we found the roads almost impassable in the little Japanese passenger car we had rented. The potholes were more plentiful than pavement and large enough for crocodiles to bathe in. We soon noticed that the locals all had the wisdom to drive large, safari-type Land Rovers, the volcano we visited shot up real fire and molten rock, and at the foot of the volcano, signs read: *Approach at your own risk.* These were not posted for Disney texture. When the earth suddenly shook for miles around, we wondered what we were doing and high-tailed it out of there. Finally, in the beautiful river where we were about to swim, where I had visions of floating lazily down-stream, we learned just in time that a very real alligator just days before had eaten a very real Frenchman's leg.

At the same time, we enjoyed a multitude of marvels: thick jungles on the edge of ocean beaches, a rare and magnificent forest at such high altitude it was shrouded in clouds, and everywhere, an extravagantly colorful riot of wild animals, birds, butterflies, and exotic vegetation. The best adventures combine risk and wonder.

No set, safe course exists for the passage through the relationship wilds. If relationship were the Amazon River, and you just were to sit passively in your carved-out canoe, powerful currents would crush you against the rocks or river banks. It is imperative to have your wits about you and to travel well-prepared. While appreciating the magnificent animals of love, also watch out for signs of danger - such as blaming, avoiding each other, thoughts about affairs, and depression. Develop your skills, pack up the best emotional equipment you can get your hands on for navigating this river - then paddle and steer very attentively.

BOOK I

Love's Five Ultimate

Truths

The Truth of Struggle and Suffering

> *Lovers know what they want, but not what they need.*
> Publilius Syrus, *Moral Sayings.*

Everyone struggles with relationship. Struggle and suffering are an integral part of being a couple. This is the first truth of love. If you are just beginning a couple relationship, you and your partner hopefully enjoy respect, kindness, generosity, a sharing of intimacy that is both verbal and physical, a spirit of discovery, passionate mutual interest, and altogether a great aliveness. Hopefully, you and your partner share conversations from the heart about your fears and dreams, a heated sexuality, and leisure and social activities in common, whether they be cooking, dancing, gardening, or reading together. For most of us, passion and connection are relatively easy in the beginning because the obstacles from the bottom of our psychological sea have yet to surface.

However if you are like most people, as your journey of relationship truly gets under way, something will slowly happen to you. The change is usually so gradual it may not be noticed at first. What causes the change will be even less noticed. But at some point you will probably wake up and realize something is very *off*. You may look at your beloved and find that their physical being, which was once so pleasing, is now less appealing. Certain previously insignificant habits will begin to annoy you. It may be the way your partner dresses, speaks, eats, or even breathes. Then their whole personality may begin to bother you: the way they are too emotional, or unemotional; the way they are overly responsible or irresponsible; the way they make, or don't, make love.

Gradually, you may no longer want to share with them what is most personal to you - or find they no longer share with you. Personal, caring, tender conversation becomes increasingly difficult, love-making less frequent and less enjoyable, and the life begins to ebb from the relationship.

The early days are so wonderful partly because new lovers are so eager to please each other, but in the process the tendency is for each to disregard his or her own needs. This is exactly what my wife and I did when we were first dating. At the same time, like many partners, we also pushed the other too far, disregarding the *other's* needs.

A few snapshots:

I want to spend the day alone; she wants to be with old friends. Instead of telling each other this, we spend the day together. At the end of the day, neither of us feel satisfied.

She likes to eat vegetarian. I like to eat steak. To be amenable, I switch to broccoli and tofu. This does not make me a happy camper.

I criticize her intelligence. She pretends my insults don't matter - and becomes depressed.

And this fuller scenario:

She comes home excited, having just learned how to meditate. (It's the late 1960's and meditation is a new import.) She wants to do it together, but it isn't for me.

Seated on the floor of our study, she remains perfectly quiet and still. After five minutes, I peek in, then pace in the adjacent room. After ten minutes, I am quite irritated. Her setting off in this new direction without me, her absolute stillness, threatens me. After 15-minutes, I turn the Rolling Stones on full volume - and she quickly stops meditating.

Typical of those days, she comes over to me almost apologetic, as if she had been wrong. Also typical of our relationship, where she tends to be more the discoverer of new possibilities, a few months later I begin to meditate in earnest, and continue to, to this day.

In that early phase of our relationship, our insecurities were so great and so unconscious, and our desire and willingness to possess the other so strong, we frequently lost all sense of our own outline, of where one of us started and the other left off. As a result we soon flipped from honeymoon to troubled waters. It took a good while before we appreciated the psychic tasks we needed to perform to get the relationship back on track.

But the key to dealing with this first phase of being together was a slowly dawning understanding: that struggle and suffering were unavoidable in our relationship, or in any intimate relationship. Most people quietly berate themselves for their struggle in relationship, especially when they feel they are failing.

Many people have a great deal of anguish and shame at how much discord or disconnection there is in their relationship. They can't imagine any other couple possibly having as much difficulty as they have, and often wonder what these acquaintances would ever think of their relationship if they only knew. To make it worse, when one goes out with other couples the other couples usually appear so well behaved.

But if you realize that everyone is struggling, it can greatly help you to relax about yourself and your relationship. Ideally it can even allow you, at least some of the time, to take the struggle with a little dose of humor. My own wife enjoys referring to the repeat-performance quality of our own squabbles as the *Jonny and Pearly show.*

In accepting the inevitability of struggle we create realistic expectations, which in turn significantly reduce our suffering. When our partnership doesn't run smoothly, when our mate fails to provide us with whatever we are looking for, or when we are less than noble in interaction, we then have far less to be surprised and disappointed about and much less to berate ourselves and our partner over. This seems especially true for those of us who are attached to being *conscious, evolved,* or simply *good.* This preference for being a mature human being makes us even more prone to lash out at ourselves when we become childishly hurt or angry. My guess is that by accepting the reality of struggle and suffering we reduce our suffering by almost half.

One couple therapist, Joseph Slavet, wrote a whole book (*After the Honeymoon*) making the very worthwhile point that it isn't arguments and conflict that cause couples trouble, but taking them seriously. He advocates that couples plan on arguments and volatility, then just move on from those situations as quickly as possible.

Once we appreciate and stop fighting the fact that being a couple entails struggle, we can go forward, which means posing two questions. First, what are the underlying causes of the struggle and pain? And second, what, if anything, can be done about them? The answers to these twin questions are the subjects of the following chapters.

The Truth of Fundamental Need & Fear

> *We want somebody to comfort us, save us, give us peace....*
> *Our whole strategic drive is for pleasantness.*
> Charlotte Joko Beck, *Nothing Special: Living Zen.*

What propels us to enter and drive through the jungle and desert of the relationship wilderness? We usually say it is because we love the other person. Biologists say it is to raise children and pass on our genes. As a psychotherapist, what I have seen is that it is a fundamental need to be loved, and simultaneously a fear of abandonment and death.

At the core of our animal/human nature is great frailty. This frailty invests us with a bottomless desire for safety and love. We *enter* relationship with this desire and at a deep level expect our partner to fulfill it. This condition then underlies all the mischief and trouble we find ourselves in during the course of our involvement. The second truth of love is that our fundamental animal/human need and fear fuel all the struggles - ALL THE STRUGGLES - that cause our suffering in relationship.

In discussing primal need and fear it is essential to distinguish our animal and human nature from our Ultimate nature. Our most essential or ultimate nature is infinite, complete, dazzlingly perfect and innately filled with love. To the degree, or on the occasion that we genuinely separate from our deep-rooted animal and human sense of being an individual self, we are free of fear, desire and therefore of conflict. We abide in the world of non-duality, of Bubar's unconditioned I-Thou.

However rarely, if ever, do most of us recognize and appreciate our ultimate, Universal, God-nature. Instead, at the profoundest level, deep in our bones, we experience ourselves as mere motes in the universe, bubbles that can pop and cease at any moment. In addition, human and perhaps all warm-blooded creatures seem to have an intrinsic need to be held, cherished, accepted, respected and valued. We then cling to whatever we can, especially to a life-partner, like a life-raft.

While existential fear and need are twin tickets we are all handed at birth, we also carry varying degrees of fear and desire from our guardians' limitations and behavior during our childhood. All children experience various amounts of disapproval, rejection or abandonment. And many of us even experience covert or even overt threats of death. These fears color the fabric of our lives, creating an underlying sense that we are unsafe. At the same time, we all know some degree of unfulfilled promises of love. During our childhood it is often just out of reach, creating an underlying craving for that need to be met.

Parental – or peer – disapproval and rejection also produces another powerful outcome. Because it is virtually impossible for children to see their parents or peers objectively, to see that a parent's or peer's rage, disapproval or disappointment relates to the parent's limitations and not to their own limitations we generally process any negative, parental experience as a message of our own unworthiness. When a parent or peer ridicules us for crying, abandons us when we get angry, or shames us when we get sexual, we assume that our natural tendencies are bad, that we are bad. When a parent or peer verbally or physically abuses us, we learn two profound lessons: first, that since even our protectors or community are out to harm us, we will not find safety *anywhere;* and second, if these all-important figures treat us poorly, it must mean we are worthless. Parents and peers are a mirror to the child, even if a distorted one.

If you look deep enough for the source of any psychological difficulty - whether it is low self-esteem, insecurity, rage, anxiety, depression or relationship trouble - you will find the same root cause: the absence of sufficient love and safety. This creates our neediness, defensiveness, anger and distrust wherever we go. Without a foundation of love and safety, our body and psyche remain in a state of trauma.

As we become adults, regardless of how successful we are, we continue to view the needy, vulnerable, *child* parts of ourselves as worthless or undesirable, making it virtually impossible to turn around and love those parts. We therefore seek love, safety and approval outwardly with the same determination with which we seek nutrients for our body. This becomes the driving force in our couple relationship. When, during the early honey-moon period, we finally feel we have found complete love and acceptance, it leaves us ecstatic. Having waited for this our whole life, we become almost addictively dependent on our partner's approval and love. No one else has ever fully loved these needy parts of ourselves. We, ourselves, don't love these parts. But finally here is someone who will. Run by fear, by desire for nurturance, and by inner images of unworthiness, and simultaneously possessing an almost bottomless yearning for love and safety, as adults we clutch our partners and expect the world of them.

Unfortunately our partner cannot possibly deliver this emotional safety-net. Partners have their own limitations, which leave us ripe for disappointment and hurt.

There is even a third way that fear and need create suffering in relationship. They actually distort our perceptions, causing us to see our partners through a veil of projections or hallucinations. Fear can cause us to see a momentarily angry husband as a monster. It can cause us to see a temporarily shut-down wife as heartless. When there is emotional turbulence we see our companion through a dream-world, making the relationship difficult to navigate.

In a nutshell, the roots of our profound need and fear are two-fold: our animal/human birthright and parental and peer disregard or abuse during childhood. The effect of need and fear is threefold: it drives us to seek more from a partner than they can ever fulfill; it creates in us an abiding belief that we are unworthy; and it distorts our view so that we cannot see our partner clearly.

The distortion and the sense of unworthiness in combination with excessive emotional weight placed on a partner almost ensure that relationships teeter or collapse. Only when we appreciate that the search for love and safety is the very driving force in our relationships can we fully make sense of our behavior and begin to give proper care to our needs. And only then can we begin to see our partner as they really are.

The Truth of Awareness

Questioner: *Master, what are the three great truths of Zen?*
Zen Master: *Attention....Attention....Attention.*

Awareness, attention, consciousness, whatever word you will, is the first and most important step we can take in making our way out of struggle and suffering. All tools and suggestions offered in the second section of this work are practical only to the degree that they are in the service of greater awareness: awareness of self and also of other. Techniques and even will-power are fairly useless in the vast wilderness that arises the moment a me and a you become intimately involved - unless they contribute to greater awareness. In fact it is not so much our needs and fears that create and perpetuate our suffering and struggle, but our unconsciousness or our denial of our needs and fears, our denial of our fundamental frailty. My wife likes to observe that she has no trouble being with friends and family who are a little *mishugina,* a little crazy, as long as they recognize they are; but people who have no awareness that they are a little crazy are impossible, if not outright dangerous.

The classic path to greater awareness is meditation. Creating a quiet, still period of time each day, even five minutes' worth, helps develop our capacity for attention. As the machinery of the mind begins to quiet, there is ever more room for awareness of both the world within us and the world around us. We can begin to pay attention to the relentlessness of the me-focus and of all the *me's* needs and fears. However, formal mediation is no requirement. The simple act of directing one's attention to the sensations in the body – the tensions, tightenings and restrictions of the breath, as well as to the thoughts in the mind, is a sufficient start to awareness.

The specific aspect of awareness most relevant to relationship is emotional literacy. In Ingmar Bergman's masterpiece *Scenes From A Marriage* the central character, a highly educated professor in a failing marriage, laments to his wife: *We're emotional illiterates. And not only you and I – practically everybody. We're taught everything about agriculture in Madagascar and about the square root of pi, but not a word about the soul.*

The first step in developing emotional literacy is actually knowing or recognizing what we are feeling. It is truly amazing how often we don't. Often we aren't aware that we are even feeling anything at all. So many feelings are frightening to have, so we simply go unconscious at their first appearance. Are we feeling fear? Hurt? Anger? Shame? I once worked with a very bright, mature woman who had been repeatedly raped by both her brothers when she was a little girl. As a result she felt tremendous shame, but it was so familiar and pervasive, like the air she breathed, that she didn't recognize the feeling as anything in particular. And without recognizing it as such it inhabited her like a demon she didn't even know existed. Noticing, naming and acknowledging the shame was the very first step on her journey to ultimately dissolving the shame. No matter how sophisticated we are, no matter how many college degrees we have, the initial steps to emotional literacy and awareness are: noticing, naming and acknowledging.

The second step is noticing and acknowledging exactly what triggers our emotions and thoughts. What precisely is it in our partner's behavior that affects us? Do we get anxious when our partner gets anxious? Scared when he is too intimate? Angry when she is distant? One day, actually three days in a row, I found myself irritable and annoyed with my wife when there seemed to be no reason at all for it: her behavior was fine and everything in my life was sailing along smoothly. However once I took time to look inward and pay attention to myself I recognized that under the annoyance I was upset with my wife because she was departing soon for a four-day trip. Although she and I periodically travel on our own and enjoy it, her leaving tapped into child-feelings of abandonment. Once this came into the spotlight of awareness the irritability dissolved, as did much of the neediness. Pascal wisely wrote in *Pensees: If men knew themselves, God would heal them.*

Ultimately we can only rely on the power and process of self-awareness and self-knowledge to maintain our footing in relationship. All humans have dysfunctional thoughts, feelings and behaviors. That is a given. But the willingness and capacity to be aware is like possessing a machete in the jungle. It cuts through the brush and creates clearings. Though it is a slow process, simply by slowing down and paying attention, by shining awareness on our millennia-old fears, needs, hurts and behavior, they begin to clear up. Only if we are conscious at least part of the time do we have a chance to survive and thrive in long-term relationship.

Denial Can Walk Off With Your Life

One flipside to awareness is denial: closing our eyes to what is in front of our nose. Often the first response to relationship trouble is to turn over in bed and ignore it, hoping it will go away. Life gets so busy and it is so unpleasant, even scary, to acknowledge that something isn't working. If we just keep moving along, looking forward, the hope is, problems will disappear. Then the more we look away, the larger the issues become.

In Jack Kent's wonderful children's story *There's No Such Thing As A Dragon,* a little boy discovers a cute little creature in his room:

> *Billy Bixbee was rather surprised when he woke up...and found a dragon in his room....He went downstairs to tell his mother. "There's no such thing as a dragon!" said Billy's mother. And she said it like she meant it.*

At first the dragon is so small that it can only cause a little mischief. However the longer the parents, who refuse to believe there is a dragon in their home, deny its existence, the larger it grows, until finally it walks off with the whole house. Only then, when there is no possible way of avoiding it, do the parents acknowledge the dragon's existence. At that point the dragon begins shrinking back down to manageable size.

Acknowledging relationship trouble goes against our self-image of being a successful, *together* person and couple. We like to look good. We like to believe we are successful. Acknowledging trouble taps into our fear that we are not so great, that maybe we don't even know what we're doing. We don't want to know in what ways we are unresponsive to our partner, in what ways we need to change. Probably more than anything, acknowledging trouble taps into our fear that the mess is bigger than we are, that it is unsolvable. The paradox is that the mess becomes bigger than us and unsolvable only when we avoid it.

Many people, having taboos or fears about arguing or open conflict, go on for years, even decades, sweeping everything under the rug. Conflict is avoided, but goes underground, causing all sorts of emotional and even physical stress. Unexpressed frustration can get pressed down and become de*press*ion, or turn into a back-ache or headache. When we don't fully acknowledge that our partner is a *pain in the neck* or a *pain in the butt,* we can literally develop corresponding pains in our body. Unexpressed annoyance with our partner can also get rerouted into irritability towards others, such as children or employees. One way or another the conflicts we sweep under the rug manage to return to haunt us.

The one path that dissolves relationship trouble is the path of awareness and acknowledgment:
Yes I am very uncomfortable with my partner's behavior.
Yes something has got to change.
Yes we need to talk, argue and fight if necessary, even get some outside help, but we have got to face this dragon, this dis-ease standing between us.

The third and perhaps most important truth of relationship is that all healing, all long-term fulfillment in couplehood begins with awareness.

The Truth of Self-Care

> *We cannot love others as others unless we possess sufficient self-love, a love we learn from being loved....*
> Judith Viorst, *Necessary Losses.*

The fourth truth of love is that the only way to tend and heal fundamental fears and needs is to nurture ourself. Once we are aware of and acknowledge our vulnerabilities, we can begin to tend them. In fact, *if you would like to resolve 99.7% of all your relationship problems,* if you would like to free yourself and your mate from your overwhelming hurts, needs and expectations, then learn how to become your own loving, accepting parent.

Parenting ourselves is the life-long task of tending our own hearts. It is learning how to nurture, comfort, love, and provide safety for ourselves, for our needy, vulnerable parts. The first step is to acknowledge just how intolerant we are of these child-like aspects of ourselves, how we tend to push away our vulnerability and neediness. In working with clients, it constantly amazes me how violently most people reject their own vulnerability and neediness. Even sweet, gentle, caring people carry a powerful injunction to reject their own neediness and to chastise themselves for having any. Many people who are very caring of their children's or their pet's neediness, paradoxically have zero-tolerance for their own vulnerability and neediness. Indeed, it is much safer to acknowledge another's vulnerability than our own. That disregard is learned in childhood in situations where it was not OK, maybe not even safe, for us to need much love or attention. If as children our innate desire for love is rejected or scorned, we ultimately cease looking for it and push it away. The tragedy is that we not only cease looking for it from our parents, we shut down our own heart and cease looking for it within ourselves. Love that could otherwise flower within us and feed our soul is stopped up.

Parenting ourselves is learning to re-access the love that is intrinsically available to us. What makes this especially challenging is that opening our heart also means opening the door to all the tremendous wounding of childhood. The only way to let love in is also to re-experience some of the pain and sadness of the earlier years, as well as some of the pain and sadness of the present moment. However, opening our hearts to ourselves makes it possible to heal those wounds and ultimately parent ourselves.

Some professionals who teach self-nurturance and many people hearing about self-nurturance confuse it with pampering, with getting massaged or served an elegant meal. Of course these comforts can be wonderful. But self-nurturing first of all means stopping in our tracks and turning our attention inward; it means nourishing on a *soul* level, rather than simply a physical or material level. This involves some very practical steps.

It helps to find a comfortable position, to take several relaxed breaths, then notice how the heart feels. If you feel ready to do this, literally note the sensation in and around the heart and chest. Is it constricted, anxious, fearful? Is it sad? Does it want love? Does it want attention? If so, can that be acknowledged? Can that be accepted? If your heart feels sad, let it be sad. If it yearns for love, let it yearn. Noticing what the heart wants is the beginning. Then if you are able to direct even a little of the love and caring you generally reserve for others at the vulnerable, child-like part of yourself, go ahead.

However, it is also important to appreciate that the early steps can be both frightening and painful. Moreover, this process is not immediately possible for everyone. If there is too much pain in the heart it may be impossible, without someone else's help and love, to begin parenting yourself. In that case, it would be wise to find a skillful, loving and trustworthy guide who can lead you towards caring for your own heart. That the guide be trustworthy and loving is of paramount importance. As Judith Viorst suggests in the opening quote, the only way we can learn how to love ourself is from having been loved. If our parents did not know how to love, then we have to experience being loved from someone, even if that means from a professional we have to pay.

The Eternal Dream

At the heart of the couple relationship is the eternal dream that our partner will *be the wonderful mother or father we never had.* We desire nothing more than that our partner give us the love, care and protection we didn't get enough of as children. We never had the perfect parents, but we are still looking for them. To the degree that our partner succeeds at this essential job, we love them. To the degree that they fail to come through and deliver the goods, we get frustrated, angry, closed, rejecting. What makes this situation so combustible is that, child-like, we throw wide-open the doors of our heart to our dream parent; when they inevitably and in any way fail to handle us with due gentleness and love we become easily and deeply wounded. Then to protect ourselves we flip into fighter-attackers, or coldly withdraw ourselves, in turn wounding our partner.

Once we can begin to comfort and nurture ourselves, once we become our heart's primary caretaker and give up the dream that our partner be our good mother or father, that our partner is primarily responsible for our care, we can loosen our demands on them and drain off the fuel that otherwise ignites emotional bombs.

Moreover, whenever we can take one step further and recognize that our partner has as much child in them as we have, that their difficult behavior is mostly their fears and needs rising to the surface, then it is easier to be more compassionate and less reactive to them.

Following is an exercise that can help to give up the dream that a partner will somehow act as your dream parent.

>Imagine that you are up in the clouds.
>Look down and see your partner with all
>their fears, anxieties and needs.

See how much *child* they have within them;
and see that there is no possibility that they can fulfill the role of being an ideal parent.

In turn, the most pragmatic way to learn how to parent yourself is to practice a visualization exercise, such as the following:

> Close your eyes.
> Pretend you are looking at a blank screen.
> Imagine the *child* part of yourself on the screen.
> Let whatever picture comes onto the screen be there.
> (The child doesn't have to look like you or in any way be familiar.)
> How does this child appear?
> Scared? Lonely? In tatters?
> Now imagine that a loving mother or father approaches the child and gives the child whatever he or she wants.
> If the child wants to be hugged, let the mother or father hug him.
> If the child wants to be protected, let the mother or father protect him.
> If he wants to be played with or just watched, let the mother or father play with him or just watch him.

Once we begin to parent ourself we can more easily unhook from unrealistic expectations of our partner. This in fact actually invites our partner to *want* to give more to us. Creating a wholesome space between ourselves and our partner, we are free to enjoy a deep mutuality with them.

The Truth of Power & Selflessness

> *Mature love is the capacity to find enjoyment in the enjoyment of the other person's enjoyment. It isn't enough to enjoy your wife's cooking. You ought to enjoy the pleasure she has in cooking.*
> Milton Erickson, MD, *Conversations With Milton Erickson MD.*

The fifth and final truth of relationship is that success boils down to combining two, seemingly paradoxical capacities: personal power and selflessness. What is more, these only arise in a genuine, healthy way after we have begun parenting our child parts.

Personal power is the strength and self-validation to freely and fully assert, when it is appropriate, our own needs and feelings. It is the capacity to take authority, to lead and to influence, to give voice to ourselves, to speak or act on our own truth. Personal power means honoring the forces of nature, the creativity, talent, sexuality, intuition, and natural authority that channel through us.

Yet, in what at first may seem a contradiction, selflessness means appreciating another's needs and feelings to be as important as our own. It means living without preferring and protecting the little me and the needs of this little me over and against anyone else. The remarkable 16th Century Zen Master, Bankei, commented to his audience: *Your self-partiality is at the root of all your difficulties. There aren't any difficulties when you don't have this preference for yourself.* Certainly, in a love relationship where there is no self-preference, there are virtually no struggles, no difficulties.

Selflessness is the capacity to bend and flow. It is the river that flows through the contours of the countryside. It is the tree that bends in the heavy wind to survive another day. It is just letting it go when our mate, in a lousy mood, becomes angry at us for no good cause.

Selflessness is giving our partner's concerns the same value we give our own. It is living without self-preference, as in the O. Henry story where the husband and wife each sell the only thing of value they own to buy the other a special gift.

While many of us rise to the occasion during the big life events, such as a mate's serious illness, it is the little situations that texture the life of the couple. One brief, indelible, marital image that has guided my wife and I for nearly twenty years occurred when another couple, then in their late 50's, spent a weekend with us. At the time, Toni and Kyle Packer had been married some thirty years, a duration that commonly leaves partners taking each other for granted. My wife and I therefore were profoundly impressed at the respect with which this couple treated each other during even the simplest activity, such as the way Toni asked Kyle for jam at the breakfast table and the way Kyle offered it to her. They displayed a deference people generally reserve for their most *important* guests, who they are eager to impress, such as the owner of their company or the Pope. Though of course who *is* more important than our beloved? Selflessness is graciously doing as one's beloved bids.

Selflessness would appear to be the very opposite of personal power. But both true selflessness and healthy, personal power rest on self-respect. And both selflessness and being true to oneself are spiritual conditions, forms of honoring God.

Selflessness and personal power are like the sea's tides. Power is the rising up in us of our fullness. The roar of the lion.

Yes! I drink up life. Selflessness is the emptying out of all self-interest. The gentleness of the lamb. *Yes! Thy will be done.*

Traditionally women, in the role of caregiver, tend towards selflessness while disregarding their personal power. Conversely men, in the role of assertive doers, tend to own their power while disregarding the capacity for selflessness.

If we exert power towards our partner without the balance of selflessness we overwhelm them, shut them down, suppress their life force, or rouse their defenses and create a power struggle, a locking of horns. Yet if we relate without our power or innate authority, our partner doesn't get to take into account our strengths, needs, visions and wisdom. We therefore rob our mate of our full presence, of the chance to rub up against us and of an invaluable opportunity to stretch and grow.

To paraphrase an old anecdote, hell is a kitchen where each partner exerts power over the other such that neither gets anything to eat. Heaven is an identical kitchen, but where each partner exerts power selflessly and collaboratively such that both eat abundantly.

The extraordinary nature of couplehood is that it functions well only to the degree that we join lion and lamb, power and selflessness, within our own breast. Long-term love relationships are therefore perfectly, some might say diabolically, constructed to inch us towards the fullness of spiritual humility. Ultimately our greatest self-interest, our partner's best interest and the true interests of the relationship are one and the same. Only when we fully step into our own power, are true to ourselves, and live in our own dignity can we selflessly honor our beloved. And only when we selflessly honor our beloved can we receive the full blessings of partnership. Only the twin vehicles of personal power combined with selflessness are capable of carrying us to enduring, mutual fulfillment with a partner.

A Few Scenic Views

Sex & Communication

Use what language you will, you can never say anything but what you are.
Ralph Waldo Emerson, *The Conduct of Life.*

Despite widespread rumors to the contrary, poor sex and poor communication do not ruin relationships; poor relationships ruin sex and communication. If communication skills made the difference specialists claim they make, then therapists and communication specialists would excel at marriage. They do not.

When I ask couples who come for help about their difficulties, often each partner acknowledges that the other was more adept at both love-making and communication in their earlier, better days. It isn't that people forget how to communicate and make love; they lose interest in trying. Likewise, partners don't tend to need much training in communication and love-making. They need help in dissolving the obstacle to healthy relationships, which is unconsciousness, and specifically unconsciousness of the deep fears and needs of the child-like aspects of the personality.

War of the Sexes

Conventional wisdom: *men and women have different needs in a relationship and have different approaches to intimacy.*
Our finding: *men and women (do not differ) in their ability to be intimate.*
Clifford Notarius, Ph.D. and Howard Markman, Ph.D., *We Can Work It Out*

It is also accepted wisdom that gender differences are a primary cause of couple difficulties. While such differences as the female tendency to work collectively and respond emotionally, versus the male tendency to work autonomously and respond cerebrally provide convenient and colorful explanations for couple conflict, they in fact play a modest role. Educational, economic, religious and every other cultural difference also plays at least as important a role as gender does. It is easy to imagine an atheistic, Swedish wife and a Catholic, Italian husband having more conflict around religious-cultural differences than around male-female differences. The gay couples I see struggle every bit as much as the straight ones. And I have watched several clients leave rocky heterosexual relationships for homosexual ones, only to wind up with just as much relational conflict.

Recently a colleague completed research proving that men and women tend to anger differently. But that they *both anger* is the significant point. It is the anger, not its different forms, that creates the trouble.

The fundamental cause of couple conflict is the exquisite fragility and emotional need that underlies all of our humanness. Focusing overly on gender only obfuscates the much darker and more difficult region in need of light: which is our all-too-human soul in its bumbling attempt to live harmoniously with another.

Why Some Survive

Whoso loves
Believes the impossible.
Elizabeth Barrett Browning, *Aurora Leigh*

Why do a rare handful of couples, including ourselves, not only manage to get through the unavoidable difficulties over the years and endure, but manage to retain a lively, respectful and joyful marriage? Altogether it seems to be a combination of simple good fortune and the following:

A thorough *determination* to make the marriage work.

Faith that marriage is do-able, largely inspired by another, older couple as a model of success.

An *openness,* sooner or later, to self-examination, to looking closely at all one's own unappetizing limitations, at one's own sorry part in marital conflict.

The use of *spiritual and emotional technology* such as meditation, prayer and psychotherapy for dealing constructively with fears, needs and differences.

Finally, and paradoxically, a *willingness to give up the marriage* for the moment, or even permanently if necessary. As important as it is to wholeheartedly throw oneself into a relationship, it is also essential in the course of a long partnership, during periods of profound stuckness, to be willing to walk away rather than spend a life in a hobbled marriage. When one knows one's partner is willing to do this, it forces one to dig deeper and change. Some wise person once commented that keeping a marriage alive requires an occasional pinch;

but the truth is it probably requires an occasional kick in the butt.

While generally the healthiest direction for righting a relationship is to dig deep into one's own inner deadness or discontent, on occasion the only way to significantly move a relationship forward is first to step away from it, perhaps dismantle it, then start fresh from a new beginning.

BOOK II

Twenty - Five

Suggestions

Frog In The Pot

Couples are a bit like frogs. Dropped in boiling water, one of these plucky amphibians will jump out and save itself. But bathing in a cold pot, with the heat slowly turned up, it won't notice the rising temperature and will ultimately expire. Couples may not physically collapse, but their spirits do, without even realizing it.

The following twenty-five suggestions are offered as an alternative to being boiled alive. They are divided into four sections representing four of the five truths of love: struggle and suffering, awareness, self-care, and power and selflessness. The truth of fundamental need and fear does not have its own section but underlies or is an aspect of many of the suggestions. In fact, although the laws are developmental, one leading up to the next, they are all to some degree intertwined.

Each suggestion concludes with an exercise or series of questions to consider. To get the most out of reading the suggestions, the recommendation is to read them one week at a time.

Reducing Struggle & Suffering In Relationship

#1 Determine What Means Most To You

> Marriage is a thing you've got to give your whole mind to.
> Henrik Ibsen, *The League of Youth.*

If love and committed relationship is not what means most to you, don't expect much to come of either, anymore than you would expect to become an Olympic gold winner, a multi-millionaire, or an astronaut without giving a great deal of yourself to the process.

Enduring, healthy couplehood is probably the single most difficult human task. Albert Einstein described making a mess of two marriages: he could deal with God and the Universe, but not with wives. Heroes and geniuses fail at it. Psychotherapists and spiritual masters fail at it. Not all of the time, but enough of the time. Relationship success requires great devotion: to the care of our great vulnerability and emotional need, to the care of our partner, and to tending the infinite, yet delicate flame of love.

If a love relationship is of ultimate concern to you, EVERY CIRCUMSTANCE THAT SUPPORTS SUCCESS SHOULD BE EMBRACED and, to the degree possible, EVERY CIRCUMSTANCE THAT INCREASES RELATIONSHIP DIFFICULTIES SHOULD BE AVOIDED.

> *Determine what means most to you.*
> What do you most want out of life?
> If you were on your death-bed, what area of life would you wish you had been most successful at?
> List your *four primary concerns* in order of importance.

If a love relationship carries the most weight...

#2 Go As Slowly As Possible

> *Spouses who marry relatively late in life...appear to have a higher average of functional marriage than couples marrying earlier.*
> Don Jackson, M.D., *The Mirages of Marriage.*

First of all, when you are in a romantic relationship, *hold off living together* until you have a reasonable foundation of trust and caring. Get to know each other as well as possible before you live together. Once you live together, *hold off getting married* until there is an even more solid foundation of trust and caring. And it may not necessarily be in your best interests ever to live together full time, or to get married. In any case, the greater the involvement - through living together, through getting married - the greater the expectations; the greater the expectations, the greater the chances for getting hurt and frustrated.

Relationships that move too quickly can easily become log-jammed and overwhelmed with problems. Taking time allows you to process and resolve issues as they come up. If in the midst of a passionate and intense relationship you quickly move in together, you can also quickly lose a sense of your own boundaries and self-hood. The price of lost boundaries is generally dissatisfaction, conflict and ultimately separation.

Enter the wilderness of coupleship one step at a time. While it is fulfilling to extend our capacities, to stretch in relationship, it is something else entirely to place ourselves in an overwhelming situation, a situation we as yet lack the tools and skills to handle.

James C., a 42-year old client, was happily engaged in all sorts of pleasant activities: cycling, hiking, dinner parties, dating.

But he was so eager to have a family that when he fell in love with a very likable young woman, he plunged in much faster than he could deal with. He pressured her to leave her home and job sixty miles away to move in with him. She pressured him to give up many of his favorite activities. They then quickly began planning a wedding. The fast pace didn't allow either to get to know each other gradually, so that they might work out differences over time. Instead, it increased the pressure to have a deep, intimate relationship. And in no time James' life was a mess of fighting and stress. With the relationship unmanageable, they finally broke off with each other.

Advaita Vedanta, a Zen-like sect of Hinduism, traditionally discourages young men and women from early marriage. Instead, it encourages them first to spend several years undergoing monastic discipline and self-inquiry. Vedic tradition appreciates that marriage in many ways is more difficult than the monastic life, and that spiritual discipline is an invaluable precursor for a successful marriage.

As a minister-colleague points out in his sermons, waiting is often essential to relationship success. If only Romeo had been willing to wait, he would have gotten the message from the Friar about Juliet - and lived to enjoy her. The slower you go and the more issues you resolve within yourself and within the relationship before you become overly involved, the more likelihood there will be that the relationship will blossom.

Go as slowly as possible.
Ask yourself: Am I in a hurry, am I over-eager
with my relationship?
If so, what is the hurry?
What is the objection to giving the relationship time to
ripen before taking the next step?

#3 Consider An Alternative

. . .

To Committed Or Traditional Relationship

> *Do you think your mother and I should have lived comfortably so long together if ever we had been married?*
> John Gay, *The Beggar's Opera.*

Many of us would be better off devoting years to developing relationship tools and practicing more manageable sorts of relationships, such as friendships and separate-abode romances, rather than to become pulled into the vortex of a traditional, committed marriage. *(If you truly love someone,* Katherine Hepburn once commented, *live next door to them.)*

If having children is your prime motivation for a relationship, explore arrangements for conceiving or adopting without a mate, and for single parenting. While single-parenting is a handful, it beats constant conflict with a partner. And some people are better equipped for parenting than for marriage. If you are getting married so that you can make love, seriously consider a more liberated approach. Enjoy love-making and leave it at that.

To enter marriage simply for the sake of sex or children is to sacrifice long-term well-being for short-term fulfillment. Neither marriage nor kids are automatically in everyone's best interest.

One couple I know wanted to marry, but appreciated that the independence and spaciousness of singlehood were equally important to them. To accomplish this, each kept their own apartment in different sections of Manhattan. What made this especially practical for them was that each was willing to give up having children. After fourteen years together each continues to enjoy their own place half the week, while living with their partner the other half of the week.

As evidence that marriage is not for everyone, many people who in later life lose their partners are *not* so eager to remarry. Once there is no child-raising to do, and the hassles of marriage have been experienced, marriage loses much of its attraction. Many mature adults enjoy a wide spectrum of activities and a broad social life without tying themselves a second time to a mate.

Friendships, a good book, travel, sports, humanitarian work are all cheerful alternatives to messy marriages - and good antidotes to the loneliness of the single life.

If you are single, dreaming of marriage, and looking out at all those *happy couples,* don't be fooled, many partners are perfectly miserable and dreaming about nothing more than getting out of the whole thing.

This is not to say that the single life is easy. The point is to do what is right and true for us, what we are ready for, as opposed to trying to fulfill a fantasy, or escape from ourselves. Instead of hurtling into marriage, many of us would be better off healing ourselves and enjoying life to whatever degree possible. In any case, coming to terms with ourselves, with our fears, hurts, and rages, produces the foundation for a solid marriage.

Consider an alternative to a committed or a traditional relationship.

Ask yourself: *Am I ready for committed relationship?*
If yes, what would the relationship look like if it ideally suited your needs? Would you live together full-time? Would you have children?

Image the exact kind of situation you would like.

See it as completely as you can, from waking up to going to work, to going to sleep.

How does it feel?

Is there anything about it that makes you uncomfortable?

If so, what adjustment would you like to make to this image of primary relationship?

#4 Marry For The Right Reasons

> To church in the morning, and there saw a wedding which I have not seen many a day; and the young people so merry one with another! And strange to see what delight we married people have to see those poor fools decoyed into our condition, every man and woman gazing and smiling at them.
> Samuel Pepys, *Diary*, Dec. 25, 1665.

If you want to enter the heart of relationship - and enjoy the abundant fruits and riches to be found there, marry for the right reasons.

When you marry for the right reasons it is as if you have already passed *Go* three times and are leaping immediately into the fourth truth of self-care. Marrying for the right reasons is taking care of yourself from the onset. It is the simplest way to limit the struggle and suffering stage and move directly towards the ultimate phase of personal power and selflessness.

First, what are some *wrong* reasons to marry?

THE WRONG REASONS FOR MARRIAGE

Because you love someone. Generally, we start out equipped only with the innocent belief that love is all it takes to make a long-term relationship work. And by *love* we mean conditional love: I'll love you *if* you'll love me. The truth is, conditional love is not nearly enough to withstand the tremendous power of unconscious forces: the hurts, fears, and rages of two wounded creatures. Love is not enough to get anyone through the wilds of long-term relationship. If this is

49

what is leading you to the alter, stop and simply savor this someone you love. Don't burden the relationship with marriage.

Because everyone is supposed to get married. People marry, even when they are not ready to, because marriage is taken for granted in our society. Despite a massive cultural shift that accepts unmarried couples living together and acknowledges that about half of all marriages end in divorce, I constantly find even among the most educated clients the persistence of the old-fashioned belief that being married is somehow the proper, mature, normal way to live, that it makes us socially acceptable.

A related belief is that, despite all evidence to the contrary, everyone else is succeeding at it. It often looks easy from the outside. The thinking goes: *if everyone else can do it, we ought to be able to succeed also.*

Because other people want you to get married. One of my clients, Daniel R., was eager to please everyone around him. A very bright, successful computer-wiz in his thirties, he was enjoying a wonderful life: mountain-climbing, jazz-playing, flying his own plane, following a fulfilling career, and living with an intelligent, lovely girlfriend. Though he seemed to have everything, Daniel came to see me in distress. Engaged to get married, he didn't actually want to be married. His girlfriend, her family and his family all were pressuring him to tie the knot. Though knowing he wasn't ready, Daniel wanted to be a good guy and acceded to their wishes.

Such pressure is tough to resist, especially if, as in Daniel's case, you are a good, obliging, conflict-avoiding person. As Pepy's quote above suggests, few people who are married actually enjoy it, yet they are nonetheless insistent that the next generation, ready or not, join them.

Because marriage and family are security blankets. Most of us have this great fantasy of wonderful, warm, caring company and shared experience. We gloss over the reality that many marriages and families are filled with little more than wall-to-wall suffering. If you peel back enough layers of image, and look closely at almost any couple you know, you will find a great deal of frustration, pain, and unhappiness. The cinema genius Ingmar Bergman writes of his astonishment while reading his mother's diary after her death. During her 40-year marriage to a widely-respected minister she had never complained. She and her husband *looked* the perfect couple. But she had been miserable from their first year. Her husband had been a cruel, tyrannical man and as a result she had suffered depression for many decades. (The director used this sad story in his wonderful film *Franny and Alexander*.)

Because marriage means ready, steady sex. This has got to be one of the most tragi-comic beliefs and greatest sources of disillusionment. Most couples leave their sexual passion at the chapel. Though many people who have not been through it find this amazing, it is common for couples to go months and even years without making love. And these are often individuals who prior to marriage were prolifically sexual with each other or with other partners. If its primarily sex that you are after – don't get married.

THE RIGHT REASONS FOR MARRIAGE

Because you are in love
and you have been together long enough to know you are compatible
and you are both deeply committed to the long-term process of knowing yourselves.

51

> *Marry for the right reasons.*
>
> Is someone more eager than you are for you to marry?
>
> If so, why are you letting them influence you?
>
> If you love your partner, what is your objection to simply dating or even living with them?
>
> Are your reasons for marriage suited to long-term commitment?

#5 Do Not Even Think About Having Children

> *Infancy conforms to nobody; all conform to it. There never was child so lovely but his mother was glad to get him asleep.*
> Ralph Waldo Emerson, *Essays.*

Until you are deeply confident of your capacity to relate under stress, do not even think about having children. Children are major stress-creators. Raising them requires a whole set of difficult skills and even then leaves most people, at least occasionally, bewildered and bedeviled. The amount of time children take greatly limits a couple's opportunities to play together, nurture each other, communicate, make love, and generally do the things that keep a relationship on a healthy keel. Children are also financially costly, which adds to the stress level.

Probably most important, children rearrange our psyches, as if they were removing one program from our psyche and adding another. Whenever children are around, good parents tend to assume *Mom* or *Dad* energy, which is a very caring, but very unsexy, quality. To take care of all the household chores that accompany childraising, parents also develop a lot of responsible *doer* energy.

In contrast, juicy *lover* energy and erotic, *sensual* energy tend to fly right out the window when *Mom* or *Dad* and *Mrs.* or *Mr. Responsibility* are around. It takes a great effort - and often getting away from the house and children altogether - to recoup them.

All these reasons are probably why a respected study found that *marital satisfaction drops 75% after the first child.* Furthermore, each additional child significantly increases the level of marital stress. When children arrive, everything in a marriage is changed forever.

Why one is having children is of profound importance. Is it to have someone to love you and look up to you? To please one's partner? One's parents? To be socially acceptable? None of these reasons are strong enough to fuel the tremendous effort it takes to succeed at both parenting and partnering.

Especially beware the trap of having children to fix or strengthen a marriage. It doesn't work. Or do you feel ready to give and devote yourself to the welfare of another very human being - while simultaneously giving and devoting yourself to your partner? If you fail, it is hell, all the way around. If you succeed, of course, it is heaven. Before you do what can not be undone, it is well worth asking all the above questions.

For Children's Own Good

For your future children's own sake, it is advisable to wait for a marriage to grow steady. When couples are in conflict, in an emotional vacuum, or in any form of psychological distress, children assume, on one or another level, the debilitating burden of caring for and carrying their parents. They will do almost anything to try to keep their parents from being depressed or from abandoning the family. Sacrificing themselves emotionally, mentally, and sexually, children can lose all sense of what they need and who they are. And when children invariably fail at the hopeless task of rescuing their parents, they absorb an anxious sense of failure that can last a life-time. A stable, relatively happy parenthood, and psychologically mature parents, are essential for a child's well-being.

Wait to have children until your relationship is on solid footing.
Ask yourself: Is my relationship truly solid? Can it withstand the gale-force winds of child-raising?

Why am I having children? What do I expect to gain?

Am I financially and emotionally prepared to maintain the lover aspect of my relationship even with children around?

Try an experiment: Borrow a young child or two from a sibling, a friend, or a co-worker and spend the weekend with them.

Then do it again the following month.

And one more month after that.

How does it feel?

#6 Develop A Solid Economic Foundation

> *It is extraordinary how many emotional storms one may weather in safety if one is ballasted with ever so little gold.*
> William McFee, *Casuals of the Sea.*

Before having children, develop a solid economic foundation.

If you are unable to save financially, then develop a career, preferably one career each, but, at the very least, one career between the two of you, that is relatively stable and secure. When you are young and in love, or simply head over heels, it is difficult to imagine how anxious you can become when you cannot pay your bills, or don't have the money to buy clothes or go out to eat. And it is difficult to appreciate how quickly this anxiety can corrode a loving relationship. Money matters. When couples lack the capacity to pay their bills, their anxiety fuels conflict. Children aside, the most stressful element for a couple is money trouble. If you marry, you should count on struggle. If you have children, you should count on even more struggle. The last thing you need to add to this mix is financial struggle. In fact a recent study found that 75% of divorces were caused primarily by financial conflict. Do yourself a favor and take care of this domain *before* having children.

Develop a solid economic foundation.
Ask yourself: Do I currently have enough extra time in my week to child-raise and maintain a lover relationship?
Can I afford the childcare that allows room for my lover relationship?
If not, what is the objection to waiting?

57

#7 Do Not Collaborate With Abuse

> *Those who stay, hoping that the violence and emotional abuse will stop, are usually disappointed.*
> Neil Jacobson, Ph.D. and John Gottman, Ph.D., *When Men Batter Women*

MINOR ABUSE

Don't confuse a partner's right to autonomy with what is part of a reasonable relational agreement. If your partner continually arrives later than promised for dinner, it is appropriate to insist he keep his word. If you are afraid to hold your partner accountable because you fear losing him, read the *Safety and Love* and *Parent Yourself* chapters. But if you can, insist your partner keep his word and he continues to disregard you, create effective consequences; the more creative the consequences, the better.

Equally important, let the consequences fit the occasion. For example, with a constantly tardy mate, you might stop taking him into account for your evening plans. Eat when and where you want, without discussing it with him. When your lover returns home enough times to a cold meal or an empty house, he will probably learn to become timely. Or at least you won't be held up and disappointed. Whatever you do, make an impression. Just the right amount.

MAJOR ABUSE

One of my clients recently described a yachting trip with her husband. As they prepared to set sail, he taught her to move quickly - by purposely pinning her leg between the dock and their forty-foot sailboat. Despite this voyage into Stephen King-land, the client wasn't sure this qualified as abuse.

If you are uncertain, but even suspect, that you are in a seriously abusive relationship, seek professional help immediately. Just as it is with the toughest prisoners of war, *the longer you are victimized, the more difficult it becomes to stand up and break out of it...* and the more difficult it becomes even to recognize that you are being abused. Don't fool yourself that it will get better by itself, or that if you just did the right thing you can make it stop, or that in some way you deserve to be mistreated. It *won't* get better by itself. There is no doing the right thing – except for leaving. And though your childhood might have conditioned you to be abused, no one deserves it.

Do not collaborate with abuse

1. Make a list of your partner's behavior that might be considered abusive.
2. Call a help hot-line (it isn't necessary to give your name) or see a mental health professional and ask for expert opinion about whether the behavior is abusive.
3. If it is, visit a mental health agency or specialist dealing with abuse.

Developing Awareness In Relationship

The light of awareness, the third principle of love, is the tool of tools for emerging out of the swamp of emotional struggle and suffering. It is the simplest of tools, for it is our birthright, yet it is also the most difficult of capacities to master. For the mind's tendency is to dodge and weave, to use denial, delusion, stupor and all sorts of other crafty means to avoid seeing what otherwise lies right in front of our nose. No one wants the pain of perceiving their own frailty, hurts and unmet needs. So though many of us pay lip-service to the great value of awareness, to some degree we all avoid it.

Arguably the finest technique for developing powers of awareness is meditation. But even in meditation we dodge and weave, seeing and experiencing what we want to see and experience and neatly avoiding the rest. My personal favorite method for gaining awareness is a combination of meditation and primary relationship. Meditation is the finest practice for honing awareness. And primary relationship is the mirror in our face that shows us our every limitation. Every reaction to our partner, every bit of anger, hurt or blame is a wonderful red-flag, announcing that within us something is murky and in need of our attention.

The following series of suggestions all pertain to facets of awareness.

#8 Don't Leave Your Partner.... If You Are Only Running Away From Yourself

> *You can bear your own faults, and why not a fault in your wife?*
> Benjamin Franklin, *Poor Richard's Almanack.*

After discovering a long list of our partner's limitations, we sometimes reach the conclusion that we have outgrown them, that maybe it is time to move on. Maybe it is. But how do we know? First, it is key to remember that all partners have their deficits. Ben Franklin's recommendation was to keep *both eyes wide open before marriage,* to look very carefully at who we choose to settle down with, then to keep them *half shut afterwards,* once coupled, to give the other reasonable latitude.

However there is another entirely different perspective from which to view our partner. Many of their less-than-perfect behaviors are simply their reactions to our less-than-perfect behavior, their defensive response to our offensiveness. If we are withholding or cool, they may act needy or angry. If we are critical, they may be emotionally or sexually withholding.

As discussed in the chapter *We Imagine Our Real Parents in Our Partner,* we can greatly exaggerate in our minds a partner's deficits when we hallucinate our parents onto them. At times, even a mate's mild behavior, say a slightly controlling quality or a relatively minor insensitivity, can cause us to project onto them a parent's long-ago, abusively controlling or insensitive behavior. We can then enter a downward spiral of excessive anger or blame, which may actually create our partner's controlling or insensitive behavior.

Whatever the explanation for our partner's genuine or perceived deficits, probably 99.4% of the times that we tell ourselves that we have outgrown our partner we are fooling ourselves. (Conversely, it is often the abused people who ought to be on their way, but who are convinced they *just need to try harder.*)

The Mad Woman & The Saint

A couple who once came to see me appeared to be the perfect example of one partner having clearly outgrown the other. It seemed that their difficulties were entirely the wife's creation and that the husband was a far healthier human being and altogether innocent. Carol entered the office speaking quickly, loudly, hysterically, and every few moments became angry without apparent good reason. Unemployed and friendless, she had spent half her last twenty-five years in psychiatric institutions for depression and alcoholism. On the contrary, her husband Richard was the picture of rationality. He spoke gently, quietly, reasonably. Easily likable, a well-respected physician with a long-term teaching position at a local hospital and no history of substance abuse or of any other significant mental health problem, he maintained that he stayed married for his children's sake and out of compassion for a wife who couldn't survive without him. Naturally, Richard's point-of-view, and everyone's that knew them, was that he had completely outgrown Carol, that he was the picture of health and she of madness. Perhaps in fact he was a saint.

The ultimate story, however, was very different. After a series of sessions, it finally became clear to me that Carol's psychiatric fireworks served as a necessary distraction for Richard. Though she certainly had a barrel-full of her own inner demons, he masked a very profound, well-hidden level of despair. Without Carol's pyrotechnics, which took his attention away from himself, Richard may well have committed suicide - as I later learned his brother had. Moreover, Richard's cool seeming-rationality, his dishonesty and self-deception, and his constant invalidation of Carol's often correct perceptions and intuitions about him and their children, helped drive his wife crazy. The doctor provided as much fuel for their marital troubles as the mental patient did. Unable to set limits with her, he even colluded in her alcoholism. Locked in an endless, gruesome embrace, the mad woman and the seeming saint were both equally responsible for their fate. (When Carol would tell people that Richard couldn't live without *her,* everyone took it as a further example of her craziness.) Appearances aside, Richard had not in the least outgrown Carol.

To help you decide whether you are truly ready to leave your partner, some useful questions are: *Am I full of resentment? Am I full of annoyance? Am I full of anger?* Does my partner really get *to me?* If the answer to any of these questions is yes, you probably aren't ready to leave. Such feelings generally indicate that we are still very caught up with our partner and have not worked out all sorts of our own issues. We may not be getting what we want, but whether we know it or not, there is something we are getting from the relationship that we need. I've seen a seemingly very independent, strong member of a couple remain in a dysfunctional relationship because, as it turned out, their scared, child part needed to be with someone they knew would never abandon them.

Moreover, a basic rule of relationship is that we have strong reactions to our partner *when our partner manifests aspects of ourself that we have not acknowledged or dealt with.* If you are fearful, but don't acknowledge it, your partner's fearfulness will anger you. If your partner is very extroverted or aggressive, and you don't allow out that part of yourself, then their extroversion or aggression will annoy you. If your partner manifests qualities that you run from in yourself, you will be angered or repulsed when you encounter them in your partner. This emotional rule is more fully elaborated later in *The Magic of Opposites* chapter.

Sometimes one partner, say Jim, will complain regularly and loudly about his mate, Jane, and even threaten to leave. Jane is so needy, so dependent. This profoundly annoys, maybe enrages Jim. Jim is tough and independent; he doesn't need anyone or anything. But nomatter how much Jim complains, he doesn't leave.

Jim may claim that he puts up with Jane because he loves her, because she just needs a little more time to change, or because he doesn't want to upset the children. But the true reason is that she expresses qualities he has not accepted in himself: his neediness and dependency. He needs to have neediness and dependency in his life: if he can't express that himself, he needs his partner to. Paradoxically, without knowing it, Jim is actually dependent on Jane.

When you feel a great deal of resentment and frustration in the coupleship, examine what qualities in your partner are especially unsettling. Are they overly impersonal and business-like? Are they ultra-emotional? Fearful? Unproductive? Once you accept and come to terms with these aspects of yourself, your resentment towards and frustration with your partner will dissolve. The issue here for Jim is not Jane. It is Jim's unacknowledged neediness and dependency. Once he accepts that part of himself, either Jane will become less so, or he will be free to leave her. In either case, the frustration will disappear.

When you stop needing some role your partner fulfills for you, and when you stop reacting to aspects of your partner that you don't accept in yourself, then you can see them clearly for who they are. Then either you simply will want to stay with them, or you will leave them without running away. Either way, the deciding becomes almost effortless.

Don't leave your partner...if you are only running away from yourself.

Ask yourself: What does my partner do that makes me want to leave?

Do I do anything to contribute to that behavior?

Does it remind me of either of my parents' behavior?

Is my partner's behavior, such as aggressiveness or neediness, a quality I push away or disregard in myself?

If so, can I begin to let some of that quality into my personality?

#9 Wake Up From The Nightmare . . . That Your Partner Is Your Original, Difficult Parent

> *Such tricks hath strong imagination*
> *That, in the night, imagining some fear*
> *How easy is a bush supposed a bear!*
> William Shakespeare, *A Midsummer's Night Dream*

The second illusion, and the flipside to wishing our partner were our ideal parent, is the tendency to *see and hear our literal parents when we look at and listen to our partner.* When our spouse behaves in ways that even remotely resemble a parent's behavior we can forget who is standing in front of us and react not so much to our mate but to our parent and all they ever did to us. The psychological term for this phenomenon is *transference.* Our mate takes on the psychological weight and fullness our parents have had for us and we ultimately invest them with all the power to hurt and anger us our parents had. When our wife makes a simple complaint we hear and experience it as our mother's incessantly critical, rejecting voice. When our husband takes a week-long trip away it crushes us with the weight of our father's abandonment. *We perpetually imagine our partner to be someone they are not.* We then respond explosively to them, which can lead to an atomic chain reaction.

Hal Stone, Ph.D. and Sidra Stone, Ph.D., developed a seminal model of this phenomenon they call bonding patterns. As they describe it, this is the arising *of parent/child interactions between any two people: the bonding of the child selves of one to the parental selves in the other. For example, the mother self of a woman may lock into the son self of a man...much the same as the bonding process that occurs between infant and parent....It is natural, instinctive and unconscious.*

Thomas S., one of my clients, is a very successful, 37-year-old college professor who develops complete mental and emotional paralysis whenever his wife, Jane, becomes even mildly disapproving. In his mind, she transforms into his overwhelming mother and he transforms into a helpless little boy. Thomas describes this as the *deer in the headlights* syndrome. If Jane simply shakes her finger at him, this otherwise dynamic, high-powered man becomes completely immobilized. Only after months of group therapy, where other members role-played his wife while he practiced standing up for himself did he even begin to get over this.

It is as if we are each programmed with holograms of our parents. Do you remember the hologram of Princess Leia in *StarWars,* who kept repeating the same words and actions over and over again? When a partner does something that even vaguely reminds us of one of our parents, we suddenly see that parent right in front of us, like some 3-D image stored in our mind that has just been switched on. And we not only lose all sight of our actual partner, but also of ourselves. The parental hologram hurtles us back decades in time, so that we become the powerless victim we were at seven years old. We re-experience the hurts of childhood and we respond with the terrified shutting down, the whimpering tearfulness or the murderous rage that were the only choices available to us back in those days.

Dorothy B., another client, is a lovely, caring woman and successful health professional who becomes a killer tiger whenever her boyfriend even raises his voice. In Dorothy's mind, her non-violent boyfriend becomes the father who used to raise a chair in the air and threaten to crack it over her head, and she becomes the twelve-year old who was ready to claw him to death.

In our work together she has found imagery techniques very helpful. Now when her boyfriend becomes angry she shrinks an image of him in her mind until he is six inches tall and no longer a threat. This allows her to feel safe and remain adult.

Another practical solution is to ground oneself in the body and therefore in the present moment. To do this, one can simply allow oneself to breathe, to follow the breath down to the diaphragm then to center oneself by placing ones attention a couple of inches below the navel and a couple of inches inside the body.

It also helps to keep reminding ourselves that this is *not* 1941,1952, 1963, 1974, or 1980, but the present moment; our partner is *not* our mother or our father; we are *not* a child, but full-grown adults, with the adult strengths and resources to protect and care for ourselves. If we ground ourselves in reality, feet on the earth, we will respond to our partner appropriately.

Hal Stone, Ph.D. and Sidra Stone, Ph.D., authors of *Embracing Your Selves: The Voice Dialogue Manual*, describe how they were originally driven to create Voice Dialogue, a wonderful therapeutic tool, foremostly to protect their own marriage. Each had been previously married and seen those relationships collapse under the weight of unconscious parent-child relating patterns. Determined not to let that happen again, they developed Voice Dialogue, an approach for bringing the parent, child and related parts of themselves into consciousness.

> *Wake up from the nightmare that your partner is your original, difficult parent.*
> **Visualize** your partner as being about six inches tall and standing in the palm of your hand.
> Take a good look at them.
> See their fears, needs, wonderfulness, and uniqueness.
> Unhook from any idea you may have that they are a manifestation of either of your original parents.

#10 Do Not Stunt Your Own Growth

> *Stretch your foot to the length of your blanket.*
> Persian Proverb

More often than most people realize, we bind and limit ourselves in order to preserve our primary relationships. Sometimes we actually *choose* to remain the same and, in various ways, encourage our partner to remain the same in the mistaken belief that this will protect our relationship. The thinking goes something like this: *Even though I am not being emotionally fed or stretched in this relationship, I won't ever leave, because I would rather be safe here with you than on my own.* Or: *I won't stretch professionally, because I am afraid I might outgrow you. And to make sure you don't outgrow me, I'll discourage you from stretching.* Or: *I won't give up my criticalness, because then you might become too confident, and that could jeopardize our marriage as we know it.*

Almost universally, marriage partners develop a remarkable, unwritten agreement: *I will live with you despite your ridiculous behavior if you will live with me despite mine.* In the process, couples limit their own and their partner's unfolding, reducing themselves to their least capacities rather than inspiring each other to their fullest. This is the prototypical frog-in-the-pot story. We enter the relationship full of zest and dreams, then let both slip away *for the sake of the marriage.*

In my own marriage, I used to have the deep, underlying fear that if I changed too much, if I became too mature, too professionally successful, if I carried my meditation practice too far, I would leave my partner behind. Then I would be all alone.

So I held myself back. For years I did not step into my full professional capacities and also restrained myself from leaping fully into my meditation. Of course when you say out loud that you are giving up the fruits of life in order to keep your partner, it sounds absurd. Nevertheless, fear of losing one's partner produces all sorts of strange, semi-conscious, self-limiting strategies. When I finally voiced this concern to my wife, about leaving her behind, she expressed the very same concern about leaving *me* behind. Fearing for our marriage, we had both held ourselves back.

It is possible to remember that when either partner moves forward professionally, psychologically or spiritually, when either partner drops some fear and opens their heart further, the other follows. Instead of the marriage keeping one static, it can become a source of leap-frogging forward.

If you suspect that you are stunting your own evolution to preserve your relationship, two things can be recommended. One, have faith that your personal development will not interfere with your relationship's long-term health. Or, if it does, you are in the wrong marriage. Two, seek professional help. In any case, as Dylan Thomas said under different circumstances: *Do not go gentle into that good night.*

Do not stunt your own growth.
Ask yourself: Is there any important way I would be living differently if I were not in this relationship?
In order to preserve this relationship do I hold myself back: Professionally? Socially? Psychologically? Spiritually?

#11 Watch Out For Roommate Land

> *Marriage is a staid and serious pleasure...and ought to be a voluptuous one.*
> Montaigne, *Essays.*

Many couples, after denying the existence of conflict long enough, enter a phase of relationship that could be titled *Roommates.* As in the children's story mentioned earlier, when the existence of a little dragon is denied it just grows larger. As the denied dragon grows, it squeezes all the passion out of the house of the relationship. Roommates might work together to keep the house running, to make joint social appearances and, where children are involved, to keep the children cared for. Many roommates talk only about the most mundane matters - and rarely if ever enjoy sex. Thomas and Miranda C., though married thirty years and sleeping in the same bed, basically just pass in the hall. "Ready for dinner?" "Umhm." They haven't made love in fifteen years and Miranda is almost always annoyed with Thomas, though she never tells him she is.

When either partner in a couple takes regular leave of their sensual-sexual energy, the couple will almost certainly drift into roommate-hood. In order to minimize the frustration inherent in roommate status, partners generally choose from several seemingly legitimate survival diversions.

Career. One's career provides an excellent and very solid excuse for being unavailable, for leaving home before dawn and returning late in the evening. Time spent with career can always be justified as financially necessary or as demanded by bosses or busy seasons. *You think I like doing all this work? I'd love to be* *home with you.* But free-time rarely materializes, and when it does, so much tension is built-up that time together is unpleasant and merely reinforces career as a more satisfying choice.

Childraising is another golden opportunity for being completely pre-occupied. Who can argue with the needs of the children?

Yardwork, house work, and **television sports events** are other popular diversions, each of which is compelling in its own way and easy to justify pursuing.

Yet the diversions are merely symptoms. They don't create the roommate-hood, just ways to safely avoid conflict and uncomfortable differences. This phase develops because both members knowingly or unknowingly collude. It takes two to be roommates. Conversely it only takes one partner to begin undoing the roommate arrangement. One partner needs to acknowledge their own part in it and their own fears or habits which contribute to it.

Watch out for roommate land.
Look squarely at yourself and ask:
What dragons am I avoiding?

#12 Assume That You Contribute 50% To All Couple Discord and Dysfunction

> *Responsibility, n. A detachable burden easily shifted to the shoulders of God, Fate, Fortune or one's wife. In the days of astrology it was customary to unload it upon a star.*
> Ambrose Bierce, *The Devil's Dictionary*

Even if it appears that it is all your partner's fault, assume that you contribute 50% to all couple discord and dysfunction. For instance, if your partner is depressed or sexually distant, ask yourself what your possible role could be. Are you emotionally distant or critical, therefore feeding your partner's depression or sexual distance? Do you disregard your partner's needs? Do you collude with a child against your partner? Do you somehow need a partner to keep their distance, so that they won't ask *you* for too much intimacy?

One of my clients constantly complained that her boyfriend was too unavailable. He kept himself busy and apart from her five nights a week.

However, when I suggested she imagine an available boyfriend, one who wanted to see her four to six nights a week, she suddenly became uneasy. She feared losing her independence and free time! Despite her dissatisfaction, on some level she *preferred* an unavailable boyfriend. (It turned out that her father was overbearing and that caused her to relish as much psychic space as possible.) If your partner is overly dependent, is it because, deep down, you need a partner who you can be sure won't leave you? Do you in fact contribute to their insecure clinging by being overly distant, disconnected, or uninvolved?

Even if you are loving, caring, and seemingly independent, if your partner is abusive, alcoholic, a chronic gambler, or devoted to other destructive habits, *your* 50% is that you are sticking around. It is easy to complain about a partner. It is easy to be a martyr. It is even easy to doubt yourself, wondering in what way you are failing your partner. The real question is, *why are you staying?* Recall the story of the Saint-doctor who stayed with his Mad wife as a distraction from his own demons. We have to look at ourselves, come to know ourselves. If you remain with someone who repeatedly abuses you or themselves, it is well to assume that you are afraid to lose them and that you are getting something out of the relationship. You may simply be insecure and need to hold on to them, or you may be unable to own certain parts of yourself and need your partner to do that for you.

We all choose partners who in some way carry parts of ourselves that we are, for whatever reason, adverse to manifest. Arlene, a sweet, caring, spiritual woman entered therapy after spending seven years with a raging, physically abusive husband. She and I couldn't understand why she had stayed, until one day she realized, as she put it, that *he was my anger.* Unable to express anger herself, and she had plenty of anger created during a very abusive childhood, she hooked up with someone who expressed little else *but* anger. In a sense, he did it for her.

If you just can't see how you could possibly be 50% of the story, take *that* as a red flag, that perhaps you need to be *right,* that you need to be the *good one.* The reverse is also true: if you consider your partner to be the *good* or *strong* one and yourself to be the problematic or weak one, if you just can't see how your partner could possibly be 50% of the story, take that fiction as a red flag. Because one way or other your partner is contributing 50% to the difficulties.

Whatever the conflict or dysfunction is about, no matter how good one of you looks and how problematic the other looks, take your focus off of your partner and learn about yourself, resolve your own issues. Each partner is always a 50% contributor to personal relationship problems.

Assume that you contribute 50% to all couple dysfunction.

1. What are the most significant conflicts or problems in your relationship?
    Write them down.
2. List three ways your partner contributes to the problems.
3. List three way you contribute to the problems.
4. If you can't see how you contribute, list the behaviors you exhibit that are opposite to your partner's troubling behavior.
    (If your partner is overly aggressive, what behavior of yours is opposite to that?)
5. Examine whether you have insecurities that require you to put up with their behavior.

#13 Attend To And Resolve Your Own Issues

> *A loving wife will do anything for her husband except stop criticizing and trying to improve him.*
> J.B. Priestly, *Rain on Godshill*

Once you appreciate that you contribute 50% to all relationship difficulty, the matter of *attending to your own issues* becomes one of the most important suggestions of all. This means staring your fears and needs in the face. Accepting and tending to them. It means examining your particular strategies for protecting your heart, which may mean that in relationship you become critical, aggressive, helpless, distrustful, distant, or closed.

Certainly, if you can keep your partner in the loop it will be to both your advantages. Coming from the heart, without judging or distancing your lover, let them know what does not work for you in the relationship. If they are willing to engage in a fruitful processing of the fears and needs you both live with, as well as explore your mutual relating strategies, that is wonderful; seek their help, share your insights.

Respectfully explaining to your partner, for example, that you feel disregarded when he tunes you out, or when he tries to solve your problems instead of just listen, or when he goes for days without being affectionate, can serve as a helpful mirror for him of his behavior. Further, acknowledging that in response you become distant and closed off can help him understand *your* reactions.

However, no matter how much you and your partner share of your issues, *the focus needs to be on your own development.* The emphasis needs to be on learning about yourself, nurturing yourself, and being true to yourself, without leaning on, making unreasonable demands of, or having unrealistic expectations of, your partner.

Attend to your own issues.
What are your deepest needs?
What are your greatest fears?
Write them down.
During the next week, pay attention to the arising of these needs and to the arising of these fears.

#14 Plan on Cycles of Withdrawal & Return

> *Relationship is a teacher. It can lead us in an exploration of both the world outside and the world within, guiding us in our own inexorable evolution of consciousness.*
> Hal Stone, Ph.D. & Sidra Stone, Ph.D. *Embracing Each Other*

Strong, enduring couple relationships seem to involve regular cycles of withdrawal and return: a pattern of connection and love, conflict, distancing, struggle, greater connection and love, more conflict in new contexts and on other levels, distancing, struggle, and further deepening connection and love. Distancing occurs when one partner purposefully removes herself from the other, whether that entails going out to dinner on her own, taking a trip for a week, or temporarily living on her own. It can also occur while a couple are in the very same room together: when a partner withdraws into herself and just sits quietly or reads a book. Appreciating that a love relationship is not linear, that it is not always going to include closeness or connectedness, makes the left turns and dips much easier to handle. When a partner physically and even emotionally removes herself, it is sometimes the only way she has to protect her inner life. During this *retreat* she has time to experience herself apart from being half of a couple, time to integrate new experience, and time to mature and develop.

The course of Susan and Nathan's twenty-five year marriage was far from straight. They met at nineteen. Though passionately in love from the start, they were too young and inexperienced to know how to maintain a healthy mix of autonomy and connection. They did not fully comprehend what *individuation,* the reality that they were each separate beings, meant. Finally, after six months of dating and living together, their underlying discomfort became so great that, without even understanding at the time *why*, they broke up.

While apart, each did some therapy, some dating, and a lot of soul-searching. The time apart was necessary for learning about themselves. Six months later, having discovered at least a little about individuation, and able to enjoy each other once more, they again moved in together. A year later they married.

But that was far from the end of the story. For awhile they were far more respectful of each other's boundaries and enjoyed each other wonderfully. Then slowly, without even noticing it, they fell into that pattern common to many couples. As Susan began to ask for more emotional attention, Nathan, feeling obligated, began to give less. And as he began to give less, Susan began to ask for more. Finally, overwhelmed by her need, Nathan completely shut down. After five years together Nathan and Susan broke up again. Each needed more time and space to learn more about themselves. After another six months of self-exploration and of gaining new perspectives, they decided they were ready to live together once again. Over the years since then, as one or the other has needed time to regenerate, they have struggled to do it without literally moving apart. Nevertheless, even as their long marriage has moved into later life, both report that they have continued to experience a steady ebb and flow: times of closeness, times of separation, and times of greater connection.

In talking to them it is clear that, altogether, these cycles of withdrawal and return have been a significant factor in keeping their relationship very much alive.

Another woman I worked with, who was enjoying a generally successful, long-term marriage, found it very helpful to spend two nights a week sleeping in a room apart from her husband. Though at first he felt rejected, he eventually supported the separation, as it quietly enriched their lives in several ways. Each savored completely following their own rhythms on those evenings, reading, keeping the lights on as long as they pleased, and each relished the quiet of solitude. Furthermore, the separation helped make the nights together more special.

Whether withdrawal lasts for moments, hours, days, weeks or even months, it does not need to signify that the relationship is over, but may simply mean that one partner needs space to breathe, to come to terms with herself and her life, and that after an appropriate amount of time the partner will return. (It ought to be mentioned that when withdrawal is done as *punishment,* it is not truly withdrawal, but a way to engage, by purposely causing pain to, the other.)

A key element of healthy childhood development is object constancy: this is the realization that when a parent leaves the room or the house the parent has not permanently disappeared, but remains a part of the child's life. It is equally important for the child to realize that *he* can withdraw from the parent's presence and still know that he is safe. (Of course the manner and degree of separation relative to the child's age makes all the difference in the world.) In order to develop a strong sense of himself, a child needs to experience physical separation as a safe, temporary, normal part of life. It does not have to imply danger or loss. Unless a child grows accustomed to an appropriate amount of his parents' leaving and returning, he will never develop healthy autonomy or independence.

Likewise, a difficult but necessary lesson for partners is learning to tolerate the other's physical and even emotional withdrawal. Healthy withdrawal creates space for inner growth and positive change, is an essential and a central aspect of all spiritual practice, and enriches both the withdrawing partner and the couple as a whole. Flesh-and-blood marriages are not linear, but involve recurring cycles of spiritual, emotional, and at times physical withdrawal, struggle, and return.

Plan on cycles of withdrawal and return.
Ask yourself: In what ways do I withdraw?
Do I do it in a constructive, non-punishing way?
In what ways do I allow myself periods of retreat?
Would I like more retreat time than I allow myself?
If so, what keeps me from taking that time?
In what ways do I allow my partner periods of retreat?

Self-Care In Relationship

The fourth principle of love is the gift of self-care. Here we turn our attention to ourself, to our own heart and learn to tend our emotional needs in a conscious, healthful way. Yet it is worth appreciating how often in relationship we simply redirect our need for care and parenting onto our partner; and to the degree that they are insufficient at this, we strive to reshape them to get them to give us what we want, or we consider leaving them. The first three suggestions of this section, Suggestions #15, #16 and #17, look at alternative approaches to the usual pattern of attempting to change our partner.

Altogether it is said that the end of all psychotherapy is to become our own fully loving, accepting, nurturing mother and father. Several key aspects to this are addressed in this section.

#15 Changing Your Partner Without Saying A Word — Part 1

> *I usually feel that there is too much effort on the part of one spouse to convert the other spouse.*
> Milton Erickson, M.D., *Conversations with Milton Erickson, M.D.*

We are always so eager to get our partner to change. If only they would be kinder, more independent, more responsible, more fun, more sexual, less sexual, more emotional, less emotional, if only they would be *different,* our life would definitely improve. After decades of failed attempts to change my wife, and of watching other partners' unsuccessful attempts to change each other, I have come to the conclusion that *the easiest and probably the only way to transform a partner is to change ourself.* As we evolve, so does our partner. Though, strangely, this secret formula is among the most difficult of secrets to remember.

A striking example of how this approach to change works occurred with a professional couple I was helping. Norbert, the husband, was so frustrated with the relationship that he was considering separating. Generally a very progressive, open-minded fellow, he nevertheless was convinced that all the marital problems were his wife Vanessa's doing. He was especially angry about her sexual and emotional closedness. Yet he didn't appreciate the part he played in being critical, pushy and unsupportive with Vanessa. She shut down sexually and emotionally in large part because Norbert was often unsupportive and frequently put her down. His own behavior helped create the very closedness he complained about. Once he discovered this, and shifted focus from blaming his wife to looking at his own contributions, he was able to start the healing process between them. Fairly quickly, as Norbert became less critical and more supportive, and without asking Vanessa to do anything differently, she became much more open and loving towards him.

Couples are in a sense a single circle of energy, like an electric circuit. Wherever you enter the circuit you can change the current. Since the place in the circuit we have most access to is ourself, that is the most effective place to enter.

The Zen of Relationship Transformation

In order to stop pushing our partner to change and instead change ourself, it helps to direct a profound question at ourself: *What is my part in the suffering and dissatisfaction I experience with this relationship?* Zen adepts ask of themselves seemingly insoluble questions called koans to plumb right through the bottom of their own hearts and minds. They might ponder for years a question such as *What is my Face before my parents were born?* Likewise, in asking *What is my part?* we open a window into an unlit room of our psyche. To get a good look, it is well to go beyond self-blame and easy labeling of ourself as *dysfunctional, sabotaging,* or *inadequate.* It is worth taking the time to truly study ourself, exploring any possible way we have helped create the situation we are in, then allowing the answer to come from the depths. The resulting awareness allows us to shift, which in turn creates the space for our partner to shift.

Change between partners also occurs in another dimension. At least that is the experience for my wife and I more times than we can count. Each of us will struggle with a related issue, say our tendency to argue. One of us may be traveling hundreds of miles away, but at virtually the same moment we both have epiphanies, resolutions directly related to that same issue, suggesting that even without discussion or proximity our efforts profoundly effect each other. Transformation is synchronous. All the more reason not to try to *force* our partner to change.

One couple, David and Rebecca, came to me after being married and loving each other very deeply for many years. They were a pair anyone would expect to go off into the sunset, happily forever after. However, they had just lost a child, something I was personally familiar with. The child's death had brought powerful fault-lines, issues they had never had to fully face, to the surface.

Suddenly both were hurting and needing lots of love. David tended not to share his crying or ask for affection. He was able to cry his heart out on his own, but not with Rebecca. He was convinced that if he turned to her, it would be too much for Rebecca; that she didn't have the capacity to care for him emotionally. Increasingly, David began to keep that part of his life separate from Rebecca. Resenting her for not nurturing him, he began to look elsewhere.

On the other hand, Rebecca began to yearn and vigorously campaign for another child, a wish David opposed. David wanted more time alone with Rebecca, to be close and to be nurtured by her; Rebecca wanted David to agree to another child. Each wanted the other to change. At a time when they desperately needed to trust and move closer, they increasingly resented each other and grew further apart. After working in therapy for awhile, David began to appreciate something that had never occurred to him: Rebecca's discomfort with nurturing him was largely a response to *his* fear of being needy with her. Though Rebecca *was* a little uncomfortable with his vulnerability, she very much wanted to nurture and support him.

Once David began opening up and showing his need for love and nurturance to Rebecca, she began to tend him in the ways he had always yearned for. When David needed caring, he could let Rebecca know, and she in turn could hold him and listen to whatever he needed to say. At the same time, David realized that his false assumptions about Rebecca were based on his experience with his mother during childhood: it wasn't so much that Rebecca was uncomfortable with his vulnerability, but that his mother had always been.

Almost simultaneously, Rebecca ceased pushing David to have another child. Instead she suggested they focus on healing the relationship, on devoting a great deal of attention to loving each other. Within a few months David, of his own, agreed to another child, and Rebecca got pregnant. When *she* changed, *he* changed. Rather than each trying to force the other to become different, each shifted within themselves, found ways to more deeply respect the other's needs - and each wound up having more of their own needs fulfilled.

It takes courage, and the willingness to be open to any possibility, even that your own behavior is less than perfect, but if you genuinely want your partner to change, the easiest, most direct route is to change yourself.

Note: This approach is *not* recommended for dealing with outright abuse.

Transform your partner without saying a word.
Take five minutes each day for a week.
Sit quietly.
Imagine you are a container and let everything wash right out of you.
Now consider the suffering and dissatisfaction in your relationship.
Having the courage and open-mindedness to hear whatever message at all is delivered to you.
Ask yourself: What is my part?

#16 Changing Your Partner Without Saying A Word — Part 2: The Magic Of Opposites

> *Every man carries within himself the germs of every human quality, and sometimes one quality manifests itself; sometimes another.*
> Leo Tolstoy

If you want your partner to become more like you - neater, more responsible, more sexual, more independent - generally all *you* have to do is to become more like *them.* If your partner is gentle and dependent and you wish they were more *assertive* and *independent* like you are, then find and express the *gentler,* more *dependent* parts of yourself. If your partner is chaotic and disorganized and you want them to become neater, more orderly like yourself, then relax and allow a little chaos into your life.

The key to this Aikido-like change-work is to notice in what way you and your partner express *opposites.* Instead of looking at how your behavior is so wonderful and your partner's is so miserable, observe how the combination balances each other out. Then challenge yourself to go in the opposite direction from which you habitually go. If you are very sexually passionate and wish your partner were also, but they instead tend towards quiet affection, then you ease up on the sexual passion and become more quietly affectionate. They will most likely respond by becoming increasingly sexual.

Three fundamental and interrelated principles account for the possibility of such magic:

1. *The more extremely one partner manifests one quality, the more extremely the other partner tends to manifest the **opposite** quality.* This dynamic produces the odd-couple syndrome so beloved of comic writers, where a Felix and an Oscar, an obsessively neat fellow living with a wildly untidy one, eternally perturb each other.

2. *We all contain the full spectrum of human qualities.* We all have the capacity to manifest any form of behavior or energy. Felix the orderly has the potential to be wild; Oscar the chaotic has the capacity to be orderly.

3. *One couple can only contain so much of any one quality.* If Felix carries all the orderly energy and none of the wild energy, there is little room for Oscar to manifest orderliness. He almost is duty-bound to carry the wild energy. However, when one mate moves towards the middle, towards, say, a mixture of orderly and wild, the other mate will also move towards the middle. As Felix loosens up, Oscar will become neater.

In the seven years Judy and Tom had been together, it always bothered Judy that Tom was not more care-free and adventurous, like *she* was. Yet Judy failed to notice that to the same degree that she was *carefree*, Tom was *responsible.* For years Judy had either suffered in silence, or complained, but nothing much helped or changed. In therapy, Judy tried a new approach. Instead of focusing on Tom, she shifted the focus to herself, to becoming more responsible - like Tom was. As she did, almost magically, Tom became more fun-loving and adventurous.

One of my favorite cases involved a corporate executive who was meticulously organized. Of course he was living with a woman who could scarcely find her way out the door in the morning, which drove him to despair. With some encouragement he created a little chaos around himself, purposely misplacing his car keys in the morning, forgetting to walk the dog in the evening, and so on. Almost immediately, his wife became more organized.

The law of opposites works like a see-saw. Whatever the issue, whether it be sexuality, money, or responsibility, if you carry too much weight one way, you will bring your side towards the ground and your partner will be lifted in the opposite direction, towards the sky. If you lighten up and start to rise, your partner's side will tip lower. If you bring yourself to the middle, level with the see-saw's fulcrum, your partner will also come towards the middle. If you shift in manifesting more or less of a certain kind of energy, your partner will likewise shift. It is a conservation of emotional or psychic energy. As a result of this happy principle, I find that even if I work with just one partner in therapy, when they change, usually the whole marriage changes.

Practice the magic of opposites.

Make a list of opposites that you and your partner manifest. For example:

Myself	*Partner*
Considerate, concerned with *other*	Self-centered
Sexually restrained	Sexually aggressive
Tidy orderly	Untidy chaotic

Visualize behaving in the opposite way from how you customarily behave.

Then practice that new behavior for a day, good-naturedly and open-heartedly.

Then observe what effect your new behavior has on your partner.

#17 Changing Your Partner Without Saying A Word — Part 3: No - Fault

> *If you want to be certain your partner will act like a bastard - accuse them of being one.*
> William O'Hanlon, *MSW, during workshop.*

When we approach our partner with a no-fault framework, it has an uncanny way of positively turning the tables. Though it is very difficult to do, it changes everything to look at relationship difficulty without laying any blame. No blame towards your partner. No blame towards yourself. No blame even towards your parents. The goal is to acknowledge everyone's part in the struggle, and to feel the pain of the struggle, but without finding any *fault*. A key element to accepting ourselves, to recognizing our fears and needs, and to accepting that we contribute 50% to relationship struggle, is doing it without finding fault anywhere.

Blaming means we step into a role of powerlessness, a victim role.
Some examples:

I'm a loser. I'll never have the life I want.
My wife's a loser. I'll never have the marriage I want.
My parents mistreated me. I'll never be the person I want to be.

Yet blame is a deeply imbedded habit that proves very difficult to undo. So when you do fall prey to it, don't blame yourself for blaming.

When we experience ourselves as helpless, our partner as hopeless, and the situation as unchangeable, we become frustrated and anxious. And when we become frustrated and anxious, we blame. Based on personal observation, fault-finding appears to be almost instinctual to humans. I have seen very young children, who to my knowledge never learned about blame, *blame* when they get frustrated. This makes sense, because blaming serves two positive functions. First, it helps us avoid experiencing ourselves as powerless. When we feel hopeless and small, we can puff ourselves up by being an accuser and trying to make the other person feel bad and small. Second, it provides short-term pain-relief. Blame diverts us from feeling the pain of the situation. When there is no blame, what do we do with our disappointment, our anxiety, our hurt? We are hurt and we don't know what to do with it. There is just raw pain, raw fear and sometimes also utter confusion, not knowing what to do. Rather than be with the raw pain, the fear, the not knowing what to do, we find fault.

If we aren't certain whether or not we are blaming and feeling powerless, certain verbal tendencies make bright red flags indicating that we are. We know we have entered victim-land when we start lobbing extreme words like *never* or *always*. "You are *never* affectionate." "You are *always* inconsiderate."

Most important, the blame/victimhood framework precludes change. When we see ourselves as small and powerless, we lose the capacity to be constructive. Meanwhile, our attacks push our partner into a defensive, shut-down posture which precludes *him* from being constructive. If you criticize your partner for being a *cold fish*, he will probably act like one.

One client regularly scolded her husband for being emotionally unavailable. Feeling judged and rejected, he reacted to the scolding by making himself *more* unavailable. *Blame maintains stuckness.* When that same client finally spoke to her husband in an accepting, vulnerable way, telling him that she loved and missed him, that the separation saddened her, he immediately became more available.

Another client was enraged that her husband treated her so poorly, of all days, on Mother's Day. Nor did he ever apologize. As Father's Day approached she plotted her revenge. However on Father's Day morning she had a change of heart, decided to let it go and treated him well. That evening he took her aside and told her how much he appreciated her kindness and apologized for his behavior on Mother's Day. Because she didn't blame, she and the relationship benefited.

Of course non-blaming doesn't mean we avoid holding someone responsible for their actions. It usually makes sense to explain to a partner that their actions were hurtful to you. The important thing is to respectfully address your lover's behavior, not attack their personhood.

However, much of the time blame is not at all about a partner's inappropriate behavior, but about their not doing what we want them to do, about events not going the way we want them to. If because it is Sunday morning I look forward to making love with my wife, but that morning she needs so much extra sleep that she wakes up too late for us to get the chance, I may feel very disappointed, even rejected. To avoid those feelings I find fault, blaming her for not being available. But she never promised to make love. Often, things just happen that we wish didn't happen. People behave in ways we wish they wouldn't. If we can allow ourselves to feel the disappointment, to feel our vulnerability around not getting what we want, we can begin to live without blame.

Hurricanes

Dealing with disappointment is just like dealing with forces of nature. When a hurricane roars through the yard and knocks down a tree, whose fault is it? Simply, certain conditions combine to create tremendous winds, then to place a tree in the line of those winds. All we can do is look at the situation and ask two questions: *Is there anything we can do differently next time to reduce the chance of harm or disappointment?* And - *What can we do now, to clean up the mess?* To protect against hurricanes, we can wire trees together, or remove overhanging limbs. Where there is no blame, we are free to act, to protect against storms, to clean up after they depart, to tell our lover what our expectations are, and to do our best to arrange for our desires to be realized. Then if our dreams are not immediately fulfilled, we can take a deep breath and *feel* the disappointment. It will pass.

Try no-fault.
Find a place within yourself where there is no blame of other or of self, where there is no victim.
Feel the pain, the discomfort, the sense of powerlessness.
Accept these feelings. Make friends with them.
Respect them.
Eventually the pain and sense of powerlessness will pass.
When they do, you will begin to find the energy to take care of yourself.

#18 Turn The Great Wheel Of Change

> *I must lie down where all the ladders start,*
> *In the foul rag-and-bone shop of the heart.*
> William Butler Yeats, *The Circus Animals' Desertion*

There is only one place where we can dependably turn around primary relationship. It is not in our partner. It is not in our relationship as a whole. Even our character and behavior are not the place to begin. The only place to dependably turn a relationship around is in our own heart.

If our efforts are rooted there, then the work we do with our partner and with our own character and behavior will be gentle and respectful. Then our lover will more likely be responsive and our own efforts to change will more likely take hold. Even if our partner remains stuck, we will be able to honor what needs to be done for ourself. And since it is impossible to know in advance what change will look like, it is important to let go of preconceived notions about where things will take us.

In the account of David and Rebecca, who had lost their daughter, when Rebecca pushed David to have another child, and he pushed against her to drop the idea, they quickly became locked in conflict. However, when each returned to their own hearts, treating the other compassionately, the situation resolved itself, in ways neither ever imagined - with the addition to their family of a beautiful child, more romance, and altogether a richer life. Only in the heart is there room for relationship to turn around.

Turn The Great Wheel of Change.

PRACTICE A MEDITATION FOR OPENING THE HEART

Find a quiet, restful location.

Sit quietly, bringing your attention to the chest and heart region.

Often it helps to close the eyes.

Allow yourself to breathe peacefully for awhile, letting the breath flow.

Feel the physical sensation around the center of your chest.

Whether it feels tight, powerful or vulnerable allow whatever sensations are present just to be there.

As you continue taking your time, breathing peacefully, feel into the softness at the center of the heart area.

Listen to the heart for anything it might have to say.

Without pushing, remain with the sensations, with the breathing, and with any opening of the heart area that is ready to occur.

#19 Have Your Own Life

> *A wonderful living side by side can grow up if close partners can succeed in loving the distance between them, which makes it possible for each to see the other whole against the sky.*
> Rainer Maria Rilke, *Letters*

Do not become glued to your partner. *Have your own life.* Let it be OK to have some separation and separate activities.

My parents, who by most standards have evolved a very fulfilling, fifty-year marriage, both love to travel, but each likes to do it differently. Formerly, their belief that they had to spend the whole day together while traveling created conflict. Each wound up doing things they did not want to do.

Their current arrangement is much more successful. My mother, who loves to walk, tours the city or countryside much of the day, while my father, who loves to sit, remains at a cafe reading and people-watching. Because each does what they enjoy the rest of the day, their time together - at breakfast, dinner, and all evening - is free of resentment and, in fact, very pleasureful.

The ultimate in relationship, the only way it ever really works, is when we have deep connection with our partner, combined with broad autonomy.

> *Have your own life.*
>
> Are there any activities you enjoyed prior to this relationship that you no longer pursue?
>
> List them.
>
> Do you miss the activities?
>
> Do you resent not doing them?
>
> Are there other, new activities you wish you could pursue, but do not because of this relationship?
>
> List them.
>
> Do you resent not doing them?
>
> What would it take to engage in those activities *while* in this relationship?

#20 Take Significant, Comfort Time Alone With Your Partner

> So they were married - to be more together -
> And found they were never again so much together -
> Divided by the morning tea,
> By the evening paper,
> By children and tradesmen's bills.
> Louis MacNeice, *Les Sylphides.*

Whether or not you have children, but especially if you do, *take significant, comfort time alone with your partner.* This is a time to regroup, work out spoken and unspoken conflicts, and nurture each other.

Find at least several continuous hours alone together every week: go out for dinner, take long walks, or do some other one-on-one activity. At least once every three months or so take several days alone together, away from all stresses and other concerns. One suggestion I make in my practice is that partners *alternate* responsibility for making the arrangements. The husband can make plans one time, the wife next time. People often complain about the expense of weekends away. There is always camping or other low-cost trips. In any case, people always seem to find money for their highest priorities. Certainly, preserving a marriage is far more important than giving children piano lessons or big birthday presents. It is also worth considering that nurturing the marriage in this way, on a regular basis, can save a fortune in therapy or divorce costs.

> *Take comfort time alone.*
> **Take out a calendar** and sit down with your partner.
> Schedule a few hours alone for this week and next week.

Circle at least one weekend over the next few months for you to get away together.

#21 Love And Accept Yourself

> *The remarkable thing is that we really love our neighbor as we love ourselves. We are tolerant toward others when we tolerate ourselves.*
> Eric Hoffer, *The Passionate State of Mind.*

Treat yourself with gentleness and kindness. Be patient, tolerant, and accepting of your limitations. *Love and accept yourself.* Remember that your fears and insecurities, your jealousies and neediness, are partly a product of your childhood, partly a product of your human nature. They have nothing to do with your intrinsic, invaluable worth.

Especially cherish and look after the needy, frightened *child* parts of yourself. Hold them, as it were, to your chest. Sometimes it is even helpful to literally place the arms across the chest. These child parts were never adequately cared for. Don't count on anyone else in your personal life to do the job. If you are unable to love and accept yourself, find someone who can help you learn how to. There is nothing more important than loving and accepting yourself. Without this there can be no successful marriage, nor fulfilled life.

> *Love and accept yourself.*
> What is it about yourself you don't love?
> What is it about yourself you don't accept?
> Can you take that part of yourself into your arms and embrace it?
> Can you take that part of yourself into your heart?

#22 Do Not Expect Too Much Of Yourself Too Quickly

> Habit is habit, and not to be flung out of the window by any man, but coaxed downstairs a step at a time.
> Mark Twain, *Pudd'nhead Wilson*

After clients have learned new tools and approaches in therapy, they often expect that they will act completely differently. I caution them that habits are not easily changed, that a habit is a well-worn path in the psyche, and that repeating old habits is the norm for everyone. Do not expect complete change. Don't waste one second chastising yourself when unwanted habits re-occur. Despite the best intentions, it is inevitable they will. On the other hand, if even for a moment you take a new path, appreciate the success. As in baseball, if you succeed at getting one hit out of every three times at bat, you have an excellent batting average.

Creating new possibilities means consciously avoiding old grooves the best you are able to. Fortunately, if you avoid a worn path in your psychic garden often enough, new growth will gradually fill in and the old path will ultimately disappear.

To transform your relationship and your life, take into account the five truths addressed in this book:

Accept that **struggle** is integral to relationship.
Acknowledge your **fundamental fearfulness and need.**
Practice **awareness** of self and partner.
Provide **self-care** to your child aspects: to the fearfulness, neediness, and vulnerability.

Own your **personal power** – and treat your partner with as much **selflessness** as possible.

Then take the key prescriptions that are woven through this book and practice them.

Figure out what **your 50% contribution** to conflict is, and pay attention to it. If you can't figure out what it is, ask your friends, former lovers or family.
Face yourself and your lover **without blame**.
Treat yourself **gently and kindly**.

And...

Do not expect too much of yourself too quickly.

Personal Power & Selflessness In Relationship

The final truth of relationship is that genuine success and fulfillment require two seemingly paradoxical capacities: the ability to act from one's personal power and the ability to be selfless in one's treatment of one's partner. In other words, we reach relationship nirvana when we thoroughly and equally honor both our partner's and our own spirit.

The extraordinary nature of couplehood is that it functions well only to the degree that we join power and selflessness within our own breast. Only when we fully step into our own power, are true to ourselves, and live in our own dignity can we selflessly honor our beloved. And only when we selflessly honor our beloved can we receive the full blessings of partnership. Only the twin vehicles of personal power combined with selflessness are capable of carrying us to enduring, mutual fulfillment with a partner.

Probably the most direct and ultimately least difficult route to thorough personal power and selflessness is the spiritual path. When we turn ourselves over to That which is much bigger than ourselves and much bigger than anything nameable, fear begins to dissolve, allowing our power to emerge, and personal need begins to dissolve, allowing us to look after our partner's interests as much as we look after our own.

#23 Respectfully Wield Personal Power

> *Self-reverence, self knowledge, self control,*
> *These three alone lead life to sovereign power.*
> Lord Tennyson, *Oenone*

To meet the remarkable challenge of being in a couple relationship, it is essential to *respectfully wield a significant amount of personal power.* To restate what was said in an earlier chapter, personal power is the strength and self-validation to freely and fully assert, when it is appropriate, our own needs and feelings. It is the capacity to take authority, to lead and to influence, to give voice to ourselves, to speak or act on our own truth. Personal power means honoring the forces of nature, the creativity, talent, sexuality, intuition, and natural authority that channel through us.

The door to the great room of personal power is the body. Power may originate in the cosmos, but it is our capacity to channel it through our body, through different energy centers or chakras, that charges us with the voltage we need to meet the needs of relationship.

The place in the body to start is the gut or belly. The Japanese call this the hara. Zen meditators, martial artists and professional athletes center here. It fuels their daunting effort. Channeling energy from this point, tiny female Akido masters are known to outfight muscular men more than twice their size and weight.

An exercise for locating this body center is to stand, feet firmly on the ground, and follow the path of one's breathe down to a point two inches below and behind the navel. Then take several deep breaths into this spot. Feel your gut and the power that emanates from there. More than just a power source, the gut is also a compass. Far from the flickering, pale thoughts, the shoulds and should-nots of the mind, the gut boldly tells us what we really want and really don't want. Even if we do not always act out what we want or feel, knowing what these wants and feelings are allows us to keep our channels open and our power flowing. We may desire our neighbor's spouse, or be enraged with our boss; but if we are unaware of these feelings, then we suppress the desire or rage and simultaneously suppress our energy. Conversely, if we tune into our gut and know what we are feeling, we may choose not to act on our feelings, but we keep the energy flowing.

The heart, the sexual area and the area beneath our sexual parts where the legs join, known as the root chakra, are also strong body centers. Tuning into these areas also allows us to locate and maintain the flow of power. Ultimately, keying into every part of the body, noticing where we might be tight and shut down, allows us to release trapped energy and recover power.

Generally, when we feel powerless it is because we are shut down, but also because we are walking around with a conscious or unconscious image of being young and small. Even anger and blame are symptoms of feeling small, victimized and, way deep down, afraid. They reflect a child fighting back.

Along with the body centers, personal power can be accessed through imaging the archetypes of power. A major one is the Warrior. A common misconception is that the warrior archetype is angry, violent, looking for a fight. Rather, it is an impersonal, fearless, all-powerful male or female figure that wishes no harm, but is implacable as protection: a master samurai, John Wayne, Superman, Wonder Woman, an Amazon.

The true Warrior, without hurt or anger, simply protects. Indifferent to fighting or not fighting, she simply does her job.

A technique for actually accessing Warrior energy, the aspect of our self that is pure strength and fearlessness, is to allow an image of a warrior to arise within the mind's eye. It could be a well-known image, like Wonder Woman, or something unique to you; whatever comes up. See the image as fully as you can. Get a sense of its power. Experience that specific sort of energy in your own body. Part of the fabric of our nature, this warrior archetype simply needs to be located and summoned.

Another power archetype is the Sorceress/Sorcerer, like King Arthur's Merlin or Castanada's Don Juan, figures with the magical powers to protect against and overcome others. The same technique described above can be used to summon this particular energy from within us. If we are open to it, we can often find our own inner sorcerer or sorceress.

When we incorporate personal power in our relationship, our needy or vulnerable, fearful child parts feel safe. They don't lead us to be untrue to ourself simply to please our partner. If a partner presumes too much, tries to push us in ways that are untrue for us, we can tell them so, authoritatively, without anger or aggression. Like Superman, our power stands gently in front of our fragile child and our partner respectfully backs away.

Paradoxically, the safety of being well-protected by our own power allows our vulnerable and playful child parts to come out and reveal themselves. More than anything, this creates the basis for intimacy and joyful play in relationship.

Wield Personal Power.

Stand up and place your palm against your belly, just below your navel.
Take a deep breath and feel the breath travel all the way down to the pit of your belly.
Ask yourself, without fear, what your gut has to say.
You do not have to act on it, but let your gut tell you what desire, need, fear or other feeling you have there.

Now feel the energy or power that comes along with acknowledging the deep need, fear or other feeling.

#24 Place Yourself In the Arms of the Universe

> *Let consciousness look after its creations! Just flow with life and give yourself completely.*
> Sri Nisargadatta Maharaj, *I Am That.*

Beyond being our own heart's caregiver, if we are fortunate enough to have religious faith, then we can depend on and *place ourselves in the arms of God, of the Universe.* As thoroughly as possible, we can give ourselves to God's care, to the care of the Universe.

At the doorway to marriage, during the wedding ceremony, most couples include a recognition of the religious or spiritual dimension, that marriage is in some way sacred. The suggestion here is to continually remember that initial impulse. Instead of looking to our partner, who is inherently as limited as we are, to take care of us, we can put ourselves in the hands of that which is Limitless, thoroughly bountiful - and thoroughly reliable. That which is *Total Mother* or *Total Father.*

Ramana Maharshi, one of the 20th Century's great spiritual masters, described deep religious faith as being like a young kitten who lets its mother hold it and carry it around by its neck. The kitten puts itself fully in its mother's care - and is completely well-tended. Giving ourselves over to the care of the Absolute liberates us from looking to our partner, and even to our limited self, to be our mother or father. We entrust the Absolute to do whatever it needs to do with us. Wherever our life goes we are tended to by the Ultimate, which really is another way to say that we turn our small self over to our Great Self.

When we give ourselves over, we allow for true selflessness, which in practical terms means appreciating another's needs and feelings to be at least as important as our own. It means living without preferring and protecting the little me and the needs of this little me over and against anyone else.

With enough faith, we can also view our partner as another pilgrim on the path, sharing our journey, but in no fundamental way responsible for our care; and as a gift of the Universe, a reflection of God, to be honored and cherished.

#25 Give Selfishly . . .

To serve is beautiful, but only if it is done with love and a whole heart and a free mind.
Pearl S. Buck, *To My Daughters, With Love*

Give what you are ready to give. Not one penny, one minute, or one ounce of energy more. Give, but only to the degree that you are being true to yourself. To do this you have to know yourself. You have to be able to separate out when you are giving for the sake of approval, for the sake of being liked, and for the sake of receiving something in return, versus when you are giving from the love in your heart. It is the same principle as giving to charity. If you give what you want to give, give no more than that, and expect nothing in return, there is no room for resentment.

In other words, don't *trade.* In trading, a person will give a thousand dollars' worth of themselves to their partner, then get upset if their partner doesn't at some point give them a thousand dollars' worth back. If you don't *want* to give, *don't.* If you do, give without expectation. Then there is no room for a rebound of resentment or disappointment. Anyway, the more we give out of love, the richer our experience and, curiously, the more we receive.

> *Give selfishly.*
> What do you give your partner that you don't really want to give?
> What makes you give that to them?
> What do you think would happen if you *didn't* give that to your partner?

...And Receive Selflessly

> *Other people...are part of the wonder that life is.*
> *They are not here to do something for us.*
> Pema Chodron, *When Things Falls Apart*

Instead of looking at a partner as something you own, someone that is supposed to provide everything, look at them as a *gift of nature:* whatever she or he gives is extra. Don't be selfish about receiving. If they give a little, that's wonderful. If they give a lot, that's wonderful. But don't look for what they aren't giving. If, on the roadside, you find a quarter or a ten dollar bill, it's a *gift.* Who would complain that it isn't more?

If your partner is dependent, yet loving, see if you can appreciate her lovingness - and be gentle with her dependency. If your partner is forgetful yet kind, see if you can appreciate his kindness - and be gentle with his forgetfulness.

Likewise, it may help to view a partner as an orchard on loan to you and under your partial care. There are seasons for fruit, and the fruit may not always be there when you wish for it. When it is available, you can enjoy and be grateful for it. Moreover, the better you tend the orchard, cherishing and nurturing it, the more abundantly, over time, will it yield its fruit.

> *Receive selflessly.*
> What do you wish from your partner that they have been unable to give, or give to the degree that you wish for?
> Can you find a way to accept that that is the best they can do or give?
> Can you more fully open to the gift they *are* giving?

Conclusion

Committed Relationship

> *Love seems the swiftest, but it is the slowest of all growths. No man or woman really knows what perfect love is until they have been married a quarter of a century.*
> Mark Twain, *Notebook*

Clients often wonder if it is actually possible to maintain the edge, thrill and fire of intimacy over years of marriage. Can the sexual, emotional and, for some couples, spiritual passion that is present at the beginning somehow be maintained? At the same time, is there a way to avoid increasing conflict?

In truth, conflict resolution, open-heartedness and enduring passion go together. Living a devoted, caring, passionate life together requires that each partner bring a great deal of courage and creativity to the relationship. It takes years of genuine, conscious exploration, which means as often as possible looking squarely in the mirror at ourselves, examining how we disregard each other and discovering how to truly hear each other. Quality psychotherapy and meditation can provide excellent, sometimes essential support for accomplishing this. But the answer is Yes. If a couple continually clears out differences that arise between them, conflict does not increase, it dissolves. Although it is quite rare in my experience to find a couple who accomplish this, lovers who perpetually acknowledge and clear up underlying conflict, who willingly open their hearts to each other, and who explore each other's spiritual, emotional and sexual frontiers, remain blessed with a robust, resonant passion that broadens and deepens over time.

It might be added that even in the most conscious, passionate relationship, intense passion is not continuously present. There is a rhythm to passion. It ebbs and flows. Every couple at times feels a kind of neutral gray. There are times when passion completely wanes, periods when the struggle to sort things out occupies far more energy than the pleasure of each other's company, even times when one's partner seems more like lead than gold. But if those neutral or difficult times are courageously faced, if a couple continuously and honestly engages in the process of shedding light on themselves, in the long run the vibrancy of the early days survives and expands.

A journalist once asked Paul Newman how he managed to turn aside the myriad, steamy young women who offered themselves to him, and instead remain faithful to Joanne Woodward, his wife of many decades. He replied that a dalliance would be like stopping for a fast-food burger when he had a fabulous steak waiting at home. Maintaining long-term passion takes a certain innocence of heart, seeing the new in the familiar, appreciating the beauty of the tree growing in your own front lawn. Then discovering pleasure in a partner, whether in bed or at the breakfast table, only improves with age.

The opportunity to share the full range of mental, emotional, sexual and spiritual experience with another person offers a wonder that only broadens and deepens with time. For anyone ready to give themselves body and soul to a conscious partnership, and for anyone with at least a degree of genuine selflessness and personal power, intimate relationship is as fulfilling and as rich an experience as life provides.

Moreover, deep partnership propels us on a journey into our own inner wilderness, through the confusion, darkness, demons and pain that are unparalleled in any other walk of life. It sends us on to great psychological discoveries and spiritual development, which is to say that deep partnership leads to a wonderful emptying out of self.

A Note On Psychotherapists

You can't choose your parents, but you can choose your therapist!
Anonymous

The primary guides to proper self-care are psychotherapists. They can be very helpful, even irreplaceable; but approach them with even greater care than you would a heart surgeon.

First, find out if the psychotherapist is specifically skilled at couple's work. If they are, what is their own relationship to committed relationship? Have they succeeded at it? Do they have a deep faith in the possibility of success - and do they know what it takes to get there? Finally, a good couple's therapist also needs to be skilled at individual work - or be able to refer you to someone who is - because it is change on the individual level that will make the ultimate difference.

Beware anyone who suggests that the problem be solved by one partner taking medication: for depression, attention deficiency, and so on. There are times for medication, but it is rarely ever the fundamental answer. In fact its use can be a misleading labeling of one partner as the problem.

A psychotherapist, by the way, is any qualified person who practices psychotherapy. They may have a degree (MSW, MD, Ph.D., MFT, etc.) or not. They may use any variety of techniques. But what counts most is the degree to which they have faced and dissolved their own issues - and your own sense of trust in them. If you have to travel hundreds of miles to find the right person - it is worth it.

Some Favorite Quotes

...his heart was going like mad and yes I said yes I will Yes.
James Joyce, *Ulysses*

Go to your bosom:
knock there, and ask your heart what it doth know.
William Shakespeare, *Measure for Measure*

Relationship can be a spiritual practice as powerful as any, combining the exploration of the body, mind and heart into a single practice.This mystical union is the fruit of a conscious, committed relationship.
Stephen and Ondrea Levine, *Embracing the Beloved.*

Sages
No more books!
No more teachers!
My wife and a few trees
Out-do sutras and sages.
Jonathan Goodman-Herrick

i have noticed/ that when/ chickens quit
quarreling over their/ food they often
find that there is/ enough for all of them
i wonder if/ it might not/ be the same way
with the/ human race.
Don Marquis, *Archy's Life of Mehitabel*

Love does not cause suffering: what causes it is the sense
of ownership.
Saint-Exupery, *The Wisdom of the Sands*

One must learn to love oneself...with a wholesome and healthy
love, so that one can bear to be with onself and need not roam.
Friedrich Nietzsche, *Thus Spoke Zarathustra*

In the difficult are the friendly forces, the hands that work on us.
Rainer Maria Rilke, *Letters.*

Suggested Reading & Viewing

Charlotte Joko Beck's books, including *Nothing Special: Living Zen* (HarperSanFrancisco, 1993).

Ingmar Bergman's masterpiece *Scenes From a Marriage.* This is wonderful in screenplay form, and dazzling in the original, six-hour video (1973).

Pema Chodron's books, including *When Things Fall Apart* (Shambhala, 1997).

Michele Weiner-Davis's *Divorce Busting* (Summit Books, 1992).

Harville Hendricks' books, including *Getting the Love You Want* (Harper & Row, 1988).

Don Jackson's *Mirages of Marriage* (W.W. Norton & Co. 1968).

Jack Kornfield's, *A Path with Heart*, a guide to meditation-awareness practices (Bantam Books, 1993).

Joseph Mankiewicz' classic movie *A Letter to Three Wives.* Starts slow but ultimately captures the pain and wonder of committed love (1949).

Augustus Napier's *Family Crucible* and *The Fragile Bond* (Harper & Row, 1988).

Drs. Hal and Sidra Stone's books, including *Embracing Each Other* (Naturaj, 1989).

Leonid Tolstoy's *Anna Karenina* (1876), perhaps the greatest novel ever written about marriage and relationship (Modern Library).

About the Author

Jonathan Goodman-Herrick, LCSW is one of the leading couples therapists in the Northeast. He also maintains active practices in transformational relationship work with individuals and groups.

After receiving his Masters in Clinical Social Work from NYU in 1985, Jonathan trained with many of the world's foremost therapists in couples work, family systems, trance work, and body work. Also having studied with some of the world's leading Advaita and Zen masters, and having enjoyed meditation for over thirty years, he has integrated an awareness practice with body-mind psychotherapy.

Perhaps his greatest teacher has been his marriage of over thirty years to an extraordinary woman. Together they have two remarkable daughters.

Jonathan Goodman-Herrick, LCSW maintains private practices in Westport, Connecticut and Park Slope, Brooklyn. For more information about working with him in couple, individual or group therapy, call 203.256.9095 or 718.768.2722.